BREAKING DOWN WALLS

Elke Hawthorne has lived an incredible life full of challenges and adventures. From her childhood as an orphan in East Germany, to her move to America as an adult, Elke's story is truly inspirational. *Breaking Down Walls* introduces you to an ordinary woman who has lived an extraordinary life!

—Drew Nichols,
Assistant Director of Admission,
St. Edward's University.

From the ashes of her lost childhood, Elke Hawthorne rises like a phoenix, finding unparalleled courage to face challenges in life that resemble the plot of a wildly imaginative suspense thriller. With Hawthorne's honest portrayal of life as an intrepid survivor in *Breaking Down Walls,* you will find yourself cheering her on and believing that she can beat the odds. By the end of the narrative, it's not at all a surprise that Hawthorne evolves into a profoundly beautiful soul that is leaving the world a better place than the way she found it.

—Sherri Defesche,
Author of *Reunion on the Rainbow Bridge: My Parents' Past Lives and the One They Shared With Me*

the child she just bore:
away. I don't want it.' It
the future ahead for this
without her mother.'
tal moaned with wake
ve, and horses could
buildings in the village
mes, still showing age
ugh the year was 1942
airplanes, the farm
female and elderly
ghts of a raging war
part included the Mit
bell tower, the
all of Mittenwalde.
oked the little village.

BREAKING DOWN WALLS

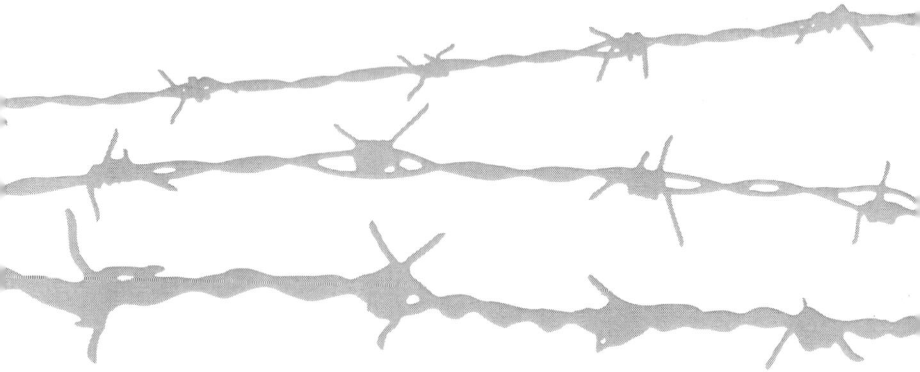

were, sometimes offered
Berlin and running the
e border crossing, most
to Alexander Platz, even
gone when their desi
or motorcycle tears were
Wusterhausen, where a
brought people to other
Wildau, Zeuthen, Eich
hof, or Berliner Zoo.

Mittenwalde. Eight
who sold fresh milk
across the street offered
ally meals. The wonder
d rolls guided everyone
ery on Jahn Platz. Fresh
grown in little gardens
Holzers were involved
ans fought all the time
stop drinking. Sundays
hildren, at twenty cents
Neumann's one of the
Schnapps or a Jäger-
the men said). For each
in Mittenwalde.

Greta carried her third
an who was serving in
eady given away before
came home for a visit
with someone else's
relationship.

's ex-fiancée visited his

ELKE B. HAWTHORNE

BREAKING DOWN WALLS

traits of a survivor

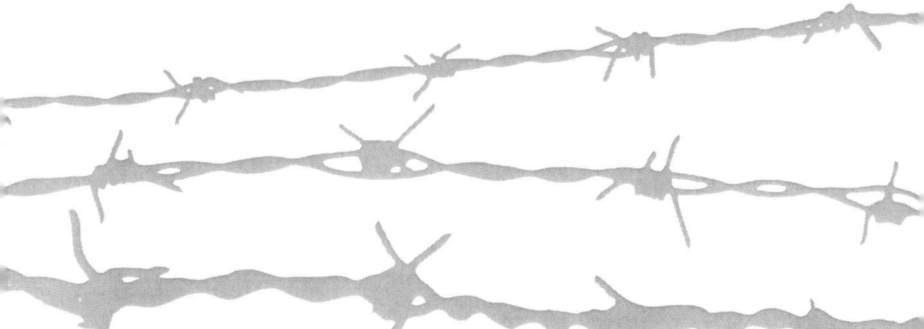

TATE PUBLISHING & *Enterprises*

Breaking Down Walls

Published by Tate Publishing & Enterprises, LLC
127 E. Trade Center Terrace | Mustang, Oklahoma 73064 USA
1.888.361.9473 | www.tatepublishing.com

Tate Publishing is committed to excellence in the publishing industry. The company reflects the philosophy established by the founders, based on Psalm 68:11,
"The Lord gave the word and great was the company of those who published it."

Cover design by Kellie Southerland
Interior design by Stephanie Woloszyn

Published in the United States of America

ISBN: 978-1-61663-368-4
1. Biography & Autobiography / Personal Memoirs
10.06.16

ACKNOWLEDGMENTS

Thanks to my mentor, Carol C. Walker, who believed in me and supported me. Thanks to Paula Marks for giving me guidance and empowering me. Thanks to Timothy E. Green, Susan C. Gunn, Karen Stolz, Nancy Schaeffer, and the Brothers Hilarion Brezik, CSC, and William Dunn, CSC, all who instilled the idea in me to write my memoirs. Thanks to Camden Frost who helped me with my cover page design. Patricia Bain, my lovely daughter and supporter. Sherri Defesche, a true friend and fellow writer. Esmeralda Hoang and Kippi Griffith—my faithful proof readers.

hand, was known as a
s having a nice word
understanding. When
in the shop she often
paying their bills, even
n sheer disbelief. Her
in a roll; her smile, her
who gave everyone the

opt me, but Greta was
Heather could have me
other financial support
new grandmother and
hteen months to three
I was well taken care of
in my cute clothes and
thing new to Heather
and gave her the sta
walk, Heather thought
eeds, collecting horse
the buggy, sweeping
Most of the vegetables
store across the street
those who had some
getting fresh fruits and
ard to get, for example
ne silks, cigarettes, and
things, so only a small
nirs made it to the fam
pared with some other
t it was still sufficient

TABLE OF CONTENTS

INTRODUCTION 11
BEGINNINGS 13
THE DREAM FOR FREEDOM 47
THE REFUGEE CAMP 57
MÜNCHEN 1961 65
A BABY GIRL 77
RENEWED HOPE 79
KEEP ON LIVING 89
A BREATH OF DESTINY 95
LOVING AGAIN 111
IMPRESSIONS 125
DEATH, KIDNAPPINGS, CITIZENSHIP 147
A TRIP TO BERLIN 163
DECISION, DECISIONS 165
A NEW START 167
FINDING LOVE AGAIN AND GLORIA 171
A VISIT INTO THE PAST 177
SPY FOR US 187
DOUBTS AND RUMORS 195
THE DAY THE BORDER FELL 199
A WEDDING 207

HOME AGAIN 211
WHAT'S NEXT? 219
EPILOGUE 221
WORKS CONSULTED 223
WORKS CITED 225

INTRODUCTION

Unique—a word that describes my experiences, which I would like to share, hoping in the process that readers will recognize their own humanity in the text. In *Breaking Down Walls: Traits of a Survivor,* I invite you to experience my personal life, which includes drama, escape, excitement, death, kidnappings, an offer to become a spy, and other strange events. My memoirs include my childhood as an orphan (so I thought), growing up in communist Germany with its hard reality, a continued dream of escaping, my realized escape and subsequent marriage to an American GI, impressions of my new country, my new family, and my new life.

gry" were her attempts
r's cruel behavior.
other loving y, had told
at these were the times
ut not heard. I knew
alk too much and stay
s' way. Now six, I had
th dark blond pigtails.
m. Omi was my only
She was a very smart
ret moments without
bout what was going on

she told me about the
rlin, and that the area
Kessel (boiler). She told
foot in the leg and ribs
uring the last days of the
being divided between
American, French, Brit
g sleep when lying in
as she kept on talking
e war had ended, these
ept there that would kee
er war again.
the Nazis and how she
sponsible for their cruel
Hitler's reign, the ruined
built up again, people
would be rebuilt, a new
be created, and that I
wear and more food to

BEGINNINGS

MITTENWALDE, GERMANY,
JULY 11, 1942

Day had not spread its wings yet. Splattered strings of peachy colors on the horizon gave hints of another warm summer day. The smell of antiseptic and anticipation lingered in the halls of the hospital in the little village outside Berlin in a war-torn Germany.

Suddenly, a baby's first outcry shattered the calmness of the early hour. In a room, Greta, a blonde, beautiful woman listened to the crying baby; and when the nurse wanted to give her the baby to hold, she turned away. "No, no, I am tired. I don't want it."

"It's a girl. She's beautiful," the nurse tried to convince the mother, but a strict "no" made her turn around and leave the room with the baby. "Such a cute, poor soul. Just born and already rejected. I wonder what kind of a life will await you," the nurse mumbled on the way to the nursery.

"How come you are bringing the baby back to the nursery?" asked another nurse.

"What do you think? She does not want the baby. She's still unmarried; one child died after birth, one in an orphanage, and now this one. She cannot take care of them."

"War times ... What do you expect?"

"At least a little sympathy for the child she just bore; I still hear her cold 'No, take her away. I don't want it.' It makes me shiver thinking about the future ahead for this little one. Maybe it is better off without her mother."

The little village outside the hospital moaned with wake-up sounds: a laugh here, a yell there, and horses could be heard from the meadow afar. All the buildings in the village looked as if they had seen better times, still showing signs of a long-ago prosperity. Even though the year was 1942, only the periodic, distant noise from airplanes, the rarity of food and clothing, and the mostly female and elderly male population of Mittenwalde were signs of a raging war far away. Impressive remnants from the past included the Mittenwalde entrance gate with its huge bell tower, the leftover ruin of the wall that used to surround all of Mittenwalde. A church with a baroque tower overlooked the little village.

Mittenwalde had several streets. There was the Paul-Gerhardt Strasse, the Puschkin Allee (the main street), the Jahn Platz, and six cobblestone side streets. Mittenwalde's environs consisted of a graveyard, a manmade lake to swim in, a little mountain, a place to play soccer, one elementary school, a main train station, a small hospital, a very small post office, and several stores.

Two small restaurants satisfied the rare visitors and the occasional drinking population. Trains brought people to Königs Wusterhausen to work and wood, coal, and iron from surrounding cities to the factories.

The separated Berlin was the closest big city (about forty-five minutes from Königs Wusterhausen).

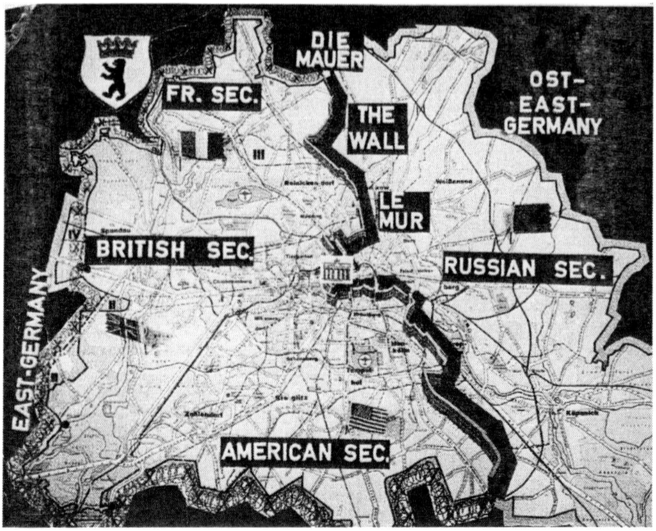

The east part around Alexander Platz, because of tourist traffic and propaganda purposes, was nicely kept up. The buildings were painted, and flowers were everywhere. Produce such as bananas and oranges were sometimes offered here. Rather than driving to West Berlin and running the risk of losing all purchases on the border crossing, most people took their chances driving to Alexander Platz, even though all of the produce might be gone when their destination was reached. A train, bike, or motorcycle (cars were rare) was needed to get to Königs Wusterhausen where a ride with the S-Bahn (city railway) brought people to other little villages along the way, such as Wildau, Zeuthen, Eichwalde, Grünau, Neukölln, Tempelhof, or Berliner Zoo.

Everyone knew everyone in Mittenwalde. Eight houses down lived Farmer Meier, who sold fresh milk from the cows. The general store across the street offered a bare minimum on products for daily meals. The wonderful smell of freshly baked bread and rolls guided everyone around the corner to the little bakery on Jahn Platz. Fresh fruits and vegetables had to be grown in little gardens. Jutta went out with Jürgen, the Motzens were involved in a dirty divorce, and the Lehmanns fought all the time because Mr. Lehmann could not stop drinking. Sundays after church was movie time for children, at twenty cents each, while the grown-ups went to Neumann's (one of the local restaurants) for a beer and a Schnapps or a Jägermeister (to calm the stomach—so the men said). For each man there were ten women living in Mittenwalde.

Everyone knew that when Greta carried her third child she was engaged to a soldier who was serving in the war, whose child she had already given away before conceiving this one. When he came home for a visit unexpectedly, he found her pregnant with someone else's child. That was the end of their relationship.

After the war was over, Greta's ex-fiancée visited his

toddler daughter in the orphanage and decided that he wanted to raise her. Greta knew that after recuperating from the birth she would have to work all day and that the father of her newborn was still in the war and married to another woman. Greta's mother, living in the poorest part of the village, took care as best she could of the baby who was named Barbara. These, then, were the circumstances of my birth. My grandmother pressured her daughter constantly to find a better solution for me. When an elderly woman offered to take me, Greta was more than happy to have found a home for me.

Shortly thereafter, Greta was sent by her doctor to a recuperation home so she would be able to work in Hitler's munitions factory again. Recuperation time meant good eating and living, for a while at least. When back in the Muna (munitions factory), Greta had to take care of finding food for herself. Stealing potatoes and coal became a necessity for survival, and in her free time she would try to satisfy her own longings for cosmetics, nylons, cigarettes, and food. When soldiers made it to the little village and she was invited to one of the restaurants in the village, she enjoyed life to the fullest. Soldiers could get their hands on nylons, cigarettes, cosmetics, and food, making it easy for them to trade for "love" when they needed it.

A tragic destiny began to unfold for me a year after I had enjoyed the love and nurturing of the elderly woman. I was abandoned again after the death of the woman and was back in the poor part of the village with Greta's mother, who had to step in again and take care of me until another place was found. One day when Greta took me with her when shopping, she stopped with me at the general store to look for shoes. The shop owner was very pleasant to me, admired how cute I was, and after this happened several times, she asked Greta if there was a possibility for her adopting me. Greta told the woman she would think about it, and she did. She thought about her options: take me and starve from hunger, or give me a future with food and clothing.

She believed that I would have a better chance, considering the material side of it all: a house, a shop, a second shop in a neighboring village, and a garden for fresh fruits and vegetables. Greta talked to her mother and friends about her decision but found mostly warning voices. Frau Heather Boller, the shop owner, came from a family that was known around Mittenwalde as calculating and cold. Heather's sister had married into the coal business, while Heather inherited the stores and the house from her mother, who lived in the same house. Contact between the sisters was almost non-existent. Married, Heather Boller took care of the store, the house, her mother, and waited for the return of her husband. He was, like so many others, fighting in the war. Greta's mother warned her not to give me to Heather, as she had experienced more than one degrading incident with her, but Greta realized that there were no other options available. It was very hard for Greta's mother to imagine me having a loving, nurturing home with Heather. She had known her a lot longer than her daughter had and knew Heather as a self-centered human being. She never saw Heather with a smile on her face, never saw her talking to anyone, and got to know her as a woman without a heart. Heather's hard features, her big stature, her bushy eyebrows, and her strong voice gave the impression of a stern woman. Most people in Mittenwalde had had some unpleasant experiences with Heather and could not imagine her as a loving mother.

Greta and Barbara

Heather 1983

Heather's mother, on the other hand, was known as a sweet and gentle woman, always having a nice word for everyone; she was giving and understanding. When she came around to help Heather in the shop, she often negotiated with the people about paying their bills, even though Heather looked on with sheer disbelief. Her mother's white hair was arranged in a roll; her smile, her intelligent eyes, and her soft behavior gave everyone the feeling of comfort and warmth.

Heather Boller wanted to adopt me, but Greta was not sure about it and agreed that Heather could have me and take care of me, promising Heather financial support from my real father. Now I had a new grandmother and a new mother. The time from eighteen months to three years went by smoothly for me, and I was well taken care of. Heather liked to show me around in my cute clothes and my nice baby buggy. This was something new to Heather.

It made her forget her loneliness and gave her the status of a savior. As soon as I could walk, Heather thought of things for me to do: pulling weeds, collecting horse droppings for the garden with a little buggy, sweeping the sidewalk, or going shopping. Most of the vegetables from the garden were taken to the store across the street in exchange for scarce items. Only those who had something to trade had the privilege of getting fresh fruits and vegetables. A lot of things were hard to get, for example: nylons, coffee, chocolate, books, fine silks, cigarettes, and cosmetics. Heather also liked nice things, so only a small quantity of fresh vegetables and fruits made it to the family table for consumption. Compared with some other children, I had a repetitious diet, but it was still sufficient.

The house on Puschkin Allee had two stories plus two cellars and an attic. A huge front door led into the garage and to the backyard. The backyard included two toilets, a wood covered septic tank, and a small covered patio, which offered a storage place for wood. The ground floor consisted of the general store, where Heather sold shoes, yarn, material for clothes, and clothing. Adjacent to it was a kitchen, a living room, and a storage room with a connection to the store and a separate cellar.

A spiral staircase led to the second floor where another living room, kitchen, and two rooms were located. The garage also had stairs leading up to the second floor to an apartment, which Heather had rented out.

From this hallway, on the second floor, a door in the kitchen was the entrance for another converted rental room in the attic. In one cellar she kept the preserves, did the laundry, and stored fresh fruits and vegetables. In the other cellar, Heather stored coal, wood, and potatoes. This cellar had no lights and the steps were rotten.

From the ground floor kitchen a small step led into the living room. Old-fashioned panel heaters had their corner in each of the rooms and had to be stuffed with wood, coal, and newspaper almost every morning to heat up the rooms. When I was about five years old, it had become my job to clean out the heaters and start a fire. Two windows in the living room looked out onto the wall of Mittenwalde's city hall, a big German Schrank (cabinet) covered one wall, and a big couch and chairs were placed along the other. After climbing the spiral staircase, a door led to the master bedroom and to a little room used especially for Heather and her hobbies. Here she would play the piano, iron, sew, and read. Grandma had her bed in this room also. On the second floor, two rooms were leased out to a family with two children, and one, in the attic, to a teacher.

When I was about three, a very tall man was holding me, talked to me, and gave me some candy. Was that Heather's husband or my real father who had come for a visit? It did not matter, for the memory of that moment stayed in my mind as a very pleasant one, giving me a sense of love, a sense of security, and a sense of comfort.

Other events were mostly unpleasant. Sleeping with Heather in the master bedroom on two single mattresses made out of horsehair, I would wet the bed very often. When I awoke, I looked to see if Heather was around, and if not, I tried to get rid of the wet sheet and replace it with a dry one. I knew what would surely happen if I had wet the bed: it was either no breakfast, a beating with the seven leather straps bound into a torture instrument or a rug beater, or having to sit in that dark cellar with the rats. The most humiliating thing Heather thought up was hanging the wet sheet out of the window for everyone to see. The more I tried to concentrate on not wetting the bed, the more it happened.

For the children in Mittenwalde, my name was soon changed to "Bed-wetting Barbara." Ashamed and hurting, many a time I made the toilet house in the backyard my escape place. It was here that I spent many hours crying.

Heather was good at thinking up new punishments for me. One of her favorites was not letting me go to sleep. Heather thought if she did not let me go to sleep, I could not wet the bed. I had to kneel in front of the bed, and when my head fell on the bed, Heather slapped me to wake me up again. Another punishment was setting the clock every hour to go use the pot or sleeping under the bed on a rubber square. Not giving me anything to eat or just beating the bad out of me, which supposedly would turn me into a good human being, were also favorites. I tried hiding under the bed to avoid punishment, hoping that Heather's anger would decrease after a while, but instead, her anger accelerated. For a while I tried suppressing my tears when she beat me, thinking I wouldn't give Heather the satisfaction of causing me pain. This also achieved the opposite, the same as screaming and crying louder and louder. Neighbors came and asked why Heather was beating me so much, but other than that, nothing was done to stop it.

Many times Heather's mother became my savior with a piece of bread or a handkerchief to dry my tears. "I don't know why she's doing the things she does to you; I know it's wrong, and that's not the way to raise a child. I didn't raise her this way."

"I think she's just bitter and angry" were her attempts at finding excuses for her daughter's cruel behavior.

Omi, as I called Heather'a mother lovingly, had told me often that I should be quiet, that these were the times when children should be seen but not heard. I knew already that it was better not to talk too much and stay out of Heather's and all grown-ups' way. Now six, I had developed into a shy little girl with dark blond pigtails, blue eyes, and an edgy disposition. Omi was my only source of love, trust, and comfort. She was a very smart woman, and when there were quiet moments without Heather around, she talked a lot about what was going on outside our little Mittenwalde.

I looked at Omi puzzled when she told me about the war that had come to an end in Berlin, and that the area where it had ended was called the Kessel (boiler). She told me about Greta, who had been shot in the leg and ribs under mysterious circumstances during the last days of the war. She also talked about Berlin being divided between the four powers, resulting in the American, French, British, and Russian sectors. Fighting sleep when lying in Omi's comfortable arms, I listened as she kept on talking about Potsdam and that, after the war had ended, these powers had created a control council there that would see that Germany never started another war again.

Omi talked about Hitler and the Nazis and how she hoped that they would be held responsible for their cruel actions. She believed that after Hitler's reign, the ruined transportation system would be built up again, people would get enough food, housing would be rebuilt, a new democratic government would be created, and that I would soon get better clothing to wear and more food to eat. At that time Omi's speeches did not make any sense to me; I thought Omi was just getting old or needed to talk. But Omi kept on talking about the end of the war and its big celebrations.

In another quiet hour, Omi would sit down with me on her lap and start talking about the first signs of the creation of a new country and a new government, especially when in April 1946, a newly formed congress stated as its goal "... liberation from all exploitation and oppression, from economic crises, poverty, unemployment, and the threat of imperialistic war. This aim, the solution to the vital national and social issues of our people can only be achieved through socialism" (DDR, 93). Little did she know that "... Walter Ulbricht's motto was 'It must appear to be democratic, yet we must have everything firmly in our grip'" (East Berlin, 14). Three years later, on October 7, 1949, the German Democratic Republic was founded. Omi told me that Wilhelm Pieck had been elected the first president of the newly founded country, consisting of 108,178 square kilometers. She talked about how the people would have to learn to live from their own natural resources, such as lignite, potash, and building materials. With an industry consisting of shipbuilding, chemical works, steel, and rolling mills, it should be possible.

The first measure of Congress in 1947 was to take away all privately owned land and give it to the farmers. The exploitive and oppressive ways of the landowners were identified as a sign of the antidemocratic former German Reich. It was decided to do away with capitalism, which those in powers determined had caused two world wars, the death of millions, and the loss of millions in monetary sacrifices. It was thought to be necessary for the Russian sector to split Germany to get away from capitalism in order to preserve communist ideals.

Factories and businesses became the property of the newly founded government—meaning the people. Private property, like Heather's house and businesses, were taken away from her, and she received a very small rent for them. From the front (war zone) came nothing—no news about Heather's husband. She didn't know if he was alive or dead. She only knew that she had to find a way to support herself, Omi, and me.

Omi, in her wisdom, followed the daily events and often voiced concern about the new ways of the new country. "They want to accomplish all these new things, but where is the money going to come from after a lost war?" Omi was wondering. She kept telling me that a new school reform had broken through the educational privileges of the ruling class by opening the doors to all children. The new welfare program would raise living standards, stabilize retail prices for basic needs, keep rents unchanged, increase old-age pensions, and raise the minimum wage.

Other times Omi told me about the health service of the GDR (German Democratic Republic), which let people consult doctors of their choice and receive prescriptions free of charge. During the first six weeks of an illness, sick pay was given, and financial support was provided thereafter. Preventive measures included sanatoriums and recuperation homes in popular forest areas and the Baltic area, not only for the sick but also for the recuperating. Some things just sounded too good to be true, such as child services that included a "baby year" off for the mother, longer paid maternity leave, loans for newlyweds, child allowances, and other benefits. "Socialism does not know unemployment and is crisis-free" became a big slogan. The defense of the newly created country was put into the hands of the People's Army, the Workers' Militia, and the STASI (State Security).

With the beginning of a new country came the beginning of new times for me as well. Those times meant no more pulling weeds, cleaning, cooking, harvesting, and collecting horse manure. Or so I thought. School started with a hope for friends and getting away from boring chores, beatings, and punishment. However, wetting of the bed went on and so did the punishments. Hiding the torture instruments or hiding myself never helped, so getting out of the house was a relief, and I enjoyed those hours. This relief did not last for very long though. Soon I found out that not having a real mother and father was a good reason for other children not to play with me—especially when this child was labeled as "Bed-wetting Barbara." Despite my hope, the punishment did not stop at Heather's house, and in school, the ruler took over. No matter what I did, if good or bad, I was punished anyway. And, to top it all off, there was Fräulein Becker, the history teacher, who had rented a room in Heather's house. Whatever I did or did not do, Fräulein Becker had nothing better to do than go to Heather and tell her about my not paying attention, talking in class, or not doing my homework. When complaints like this came, Heather thought I needed more to do; this way I would not talk in class and would pay attention. I remember the time when I had forgotten to do one assignment. After Fräulein Becker had left, Heather got in a fury, took scissors, and cut my pigtails off, right at the beginning, close to my head. I still cried the next day going to school and all day in school.

After the new government had taken Heather's property and stores away from her, she was forced to find something else to do. She had to move from downstairs to upstairs and had fewer rooms for herself. The little money she received for the use of the house and stores every month could not support her needs. She soon found a job delivering mail to the population of Mittenwalde and surrounding houses.

Around that time my only support, love, understanding, and hope was taken away. Omi had fallen from the spiral staircase and had broken her hip. She was eighty-two, and the doctor warned us that her hip might never heal again. Every chance I had was spent with Omi, lying beside her, talking to her, letting her know that she was not alone, that she was loved so much, and that I could not live without her. But soon I had to learn to live without my beloved Omi. I was lying in bed beside her one Saturday afternoon when my beloved Omi went to sleep forever. Heather got a casket, and Omi was stored on stilts in the covered driveway. Minka, the cat, did not eat or move for three days until Omi was picked up by the funeral home. My days were spent in a trance. I could not understand how the only person in the world who cared about me, my only connection to love, my life, could have left me. I walked around in shock, without tears, emotionless, and without a goal, just getting through the days, not caring how, or with whom. At the funeral, I was told later I had behaved unreasonably by throwing myself on the casket screaming for Omi. My memory of these days stayed locked up, and it took a very long time before I could even mention the name "Omi" to anyone.

A new job for Heather required new duties for me:

cook in a hurry when coming from school and have the food on the table at exactly noon, when Heather stopped by to eat her lunch. Unfortunately for me, sometimes the food was not ready.

Minka just had kittens again, and it was a lot more interesting to play with the little ones than to cook and clean. In addition to working in the garden, cooking, doing homework for school, and cleaning the house, another chore was added: delivering the mail to the areas surrounding Mittenwalde by bicycle. When the weather was nice, I did not mind doing it; I liked bicycling, but when it rained, it was almost dark during the daytime, and riding through the forest on the way back was spooky and scary. Sometimes I thought I saw the shadow of a disfigured man running from tree to tree, and other times I heard a howling and growling, twigs breaking, and sounds of whispering. Fortunately, most of the forests around Mittenwalde were familiar to me from the times I had to collect pinecones to fire up the panel heaters in the mornings. When I was scared riding through the forest, I tried to think of happier times, tried to find distraction, and found it usually thinking of the newly found friendship that had presented itself next door.

A neighbor, Grandma Bethke (who, by the way, made very good cookies and sandwiches), had two grandchildren, who came to visit every now and then. They lived in Königs Wusterhausen with their parents. Wanda, Grandma Bethke's granddaughter, became my only friend whenever she was in town.

Wanda and Barbara

Wanda's brother Wolfgang was seldom around, and if he was, brother and sister kept fighting. I wanted only to be with Wanda. She helped me finish the chores so that we could play for a while, but Wanda did not come around when Heather was there. The horror stories Wanda had heard from her grandmother about Heather made her afraid of her.

Before school, my everyday chores included getting the panel heaters going to heat up the house, going to Farmer Meier to get fresh milk and walking around the corner for fresh Brötchen (split rolls). One morning at Farmer Meier's house, I could not resist a young kitten running right in front of the doghouse. When running after it, I did not consider the long chain on that vicious dog. It stormed out and grabbed me right at the ribs and shook me around like a rag doll. Mr. Meier came running and hit the dog to make it let go of me. Heather was summoned to get her daughter, and all the way to the doctor, Heather hit me for my stupidity. After several stitches, a shot, and many tears, I was released into Heather's care again. The days went on with the same daily chores and punishments.

The new government also made itself felt in my life. In school, hours were set aside for the young pioneers (Junge Pioniere), a youth group that was taught synchronized marching for showing enthusiasm at political events, holiday celebrations, and when heads of other governments visited. They also had to help farmers pick potato bugs in the field or harvest. The teachers repeatedly talked about how bad capitalism was, that socialism was the only good kind of government, and that listening to radio stations other than German Democratic Republic stations was considered treason and would be punished with imprisonment. The Free German Youth (Freie Deutsche Jugend) came next; participation in each group was mandatory, and each had their own special uniforms. The Free German Youth also had to help where help was necessary, bringing in hay, cleaning, and participating in marches for the GDR (German Democratic Republic). Assembly of more than three people was forbidden, and Western television stations (if they could be received) were off limits.

People who did not live up to these rules needed to be reported, which meant a fast pickup by the STASI and imprisonment for the whole family. In school, new classes were added, including entrance into socialist production, productive work, nationality teaching, and astronomy. Twice a week I had classes for religious studies in the evening, and once a week Arbeiterdienst (work duty). The classes in school included German language and literature, mathematics, Russian, physics, biology, chemistry, geography, history, art, music, physical therapy, needlework, and current socialist teachings. Besides the Russian language (which was mandatory), English and French showed up on the report cards, but were never offered. The years followed one after another.

At the age of twelve, I had a visitor again: Greta. She had visited before in intervals of a year or two. She came to see how I was doing. She explained to me that she was my real mother and that she stayed with my real grandmother in the poor housing area in Mittenwalde. She told me that I could go visit her but that I could not stay with my real grandmother. I wanted to leave with Greta and told her about the punishment and the beatings, and that the only love I had ever received was from Omi. Greta, not believing me, left again. She hugged me and told me that she loved me but could not take me with her; she went, leaving behind an angry, sad, and confused me. These repeated visits were very much rejected by Heather. She kept pointing out that she was my real mother, keeping me fed, warm, healthy and that Greta was just a prostitute messing around with the Russians. She told me that Greta never paid any money to support me and that she could throw me out on the streets if she wanted to. Nevertheless, I looked forward to Greta's visits, which at least, sometimes, brought me a new outfit or some sweets. Otherwise, I felt torn between the two women, not knowing which one told the truth, wondering who really my real mother was.

Greta

Another short visit from Greta with a picture-taking session

Omi had been the one who always answered my questions truthfully, and she had once told me that Greta was my real mother. The pleas to Greta to take me with her got more intense in the years that followed, but they remained unsuccessful. Every now and then, I tried hiding out with my real grandmother, but Heather always found me, and my grandmother also encouraged me to go back to her. She explained that she was sick and had a very short supply of food and other necessities, unable to take care of a child.

The days went on in monotony, consisting of getting up at six, heating the rooms, getting milk and rolls, fixing breakfast, going to school, getting home to start the cooking, cleaning up, and doing homework for school. When Heather came home, she went with me to the garden to pull weeds, harvest, and plant. The bedwetting was still going on, as were the beatings.

One day, Wanda came to visit and wanted to play with me, but I had a lot of chores to finish and could not play. Angry, I felt my emotions running astray, and I wanted only to get back at Heather, to hurt her just once for all the times of abuse, one time I wanted revenge, to give back some of the hurt I had felt for years. In the backyard toilet house, I hatched out a plan considering Heather's weakness: money. The next time I was asked to harvest fruits in the garden, I told four schoolmates to join me. We all climbed into the plum tree and started eating away. When we were full, we started shaking the tree so that all the plums would fall down and be unusable. For days I had a hard time finding a comfortable spot to sit on in the school's chair; nevertheless, it was a satisfying experience to me.

Other enjoyable moments in my life included the days when Heather went to Berlin for a couple of days. She went to visit a lady friend at Kotbusser Damm and, as I found out later, also to meet with a boyfriend. These days meant having fun, not being afraid, playing with the cats, exploring the attic for strange items, not doing my chores, watching people, and enjoying the brief moments of freedom. Wanda and Wolfgang had come for a visit again. It was wintertime, and we all went ice-skating on a frozen-over field that was close to the lake. We even enjoyed falling and getting up again, until suddenly Wanda started screaming "Help, help me!" The ice had broken from beneath her, and even though she could not sink deep on the frozen-over field, she was scared. My first instinct was to run because I thought I had done something wrong again, but Wolfgang helped Wanda out and took her home. She got very sick from getting wet, and I felt very bad about it for a long time, thinking it was, like always, my fault. Wanda and Wolfgang introduced me to something brand new—a birthday party! Wanda had invited me to my first birthday party. Wanda had looked at me very puzzled when she had to explain what a birthday party was—that you get presents, a cake with candles, balloons, and you celebrate with friends and family. After an afternoon of eating cake, singing, and playing, I also wanted to have a birthday party, a wish that was never realized.

Once, Heather took me with her to her lady friend in Berlin. For the first time in my life, I saw a person with a hunchback. In my mind I thought Heather was going to sell me to the "witch." The lady had a black cat that did not like children, and every time I went by the bed in the bedroom, it would jump out and scratch my legs. After being there several times, I felt that I had to get back at that cat. When cleaning the apartment for the lady, I used the vacuum cleaner to scare the cat and get her out from under the bed. She got so scared that she jumped on top of an old cabinet and stayed there until the lady came back. Needless to say, I did not have to clean that lady's apartment any more because I had scared her precious cat. My punishment consisted of some extra chores when we got home. Another friend of Heather, who did some sewing for her, was the opposite from the hunchback. This lady was beautiful, even though in my eyes she was very old (forty-five). She treated me very kindly and gave me candy and books to read. In one of them I had found a map of all Berlin, East and West, which I put in my dress she had altered and took home, not knowing at this time that this map would play a very important part in my future.

Travel to and from Berlin was easy at that time. Only a toll bar and a little covered house for the soldiers separated East Berlin from West Berlin, and if the S-Bahn (city railway) was used, a guard checked everyone's papers. When somebody looked suspicious, they would have to get off the train, and the guard would confiscate whatever they liked and keep it for themselves. It was forbidden to import certain things, such as books, which were considered slanderous and dangerous to the GDR. It was forbidden to import clothing with a strong Western look such as jeans or anything that had to do with war, such as toy soldiers, toy tanks, or toy guns, and especially daily newspapers or magazines from the West.

I was fourteen now, at an age where children in school started wearing only certain things—and the Western look was in. Petticoats and jeans, chewing gum, and the

"Hit Parade" records became hot items. Secretly and quietly we sung "Johnny B. Goode," "Love Potion No. 9," "Dream Lover," or "Chantilly Lace," which had played on the "Hit Parade." Over the years I had accumulated my own little treasure, putting away money I had gotten from my Omi and money I had earned doing odd jobs for some of Mittenwalde's population. My new worry became how to find ways to get these hot items. When I had the chance to get to Berlin, I wore a regular dress and came back with a petticoat under it. That was one of the easiest things to get out of West Berlin. Another time I wore regular pants, but under them I was hiding a new pair of jeans. One time I got caught because the new jeans peeked out from under my regular pants. I lost that pair of jeans and everything else I had bought that day, but it taught me a lesson to be more careful the next time.

In Mittenwalde, more and more houses were becoming vacant. From one day to another children I had seen in school were gone. When I asked about them I was told they were picked up by the Stasi (State Security) for actions against the government or had left for refugee camps in West Berlin never to return. I registered it, but other things were more important at this time like my secret meetings on Tone Mountain with two other teenagers. The fact that we ran the danger of being arrested when caught made listening to our radio program from the West even more precious. It was then that we heard news about new refugee camps being opened because the old ones were overcrowded. It was 1958, an important time for me because I finished eight grades, which concluded all the education Heather would provide for me.

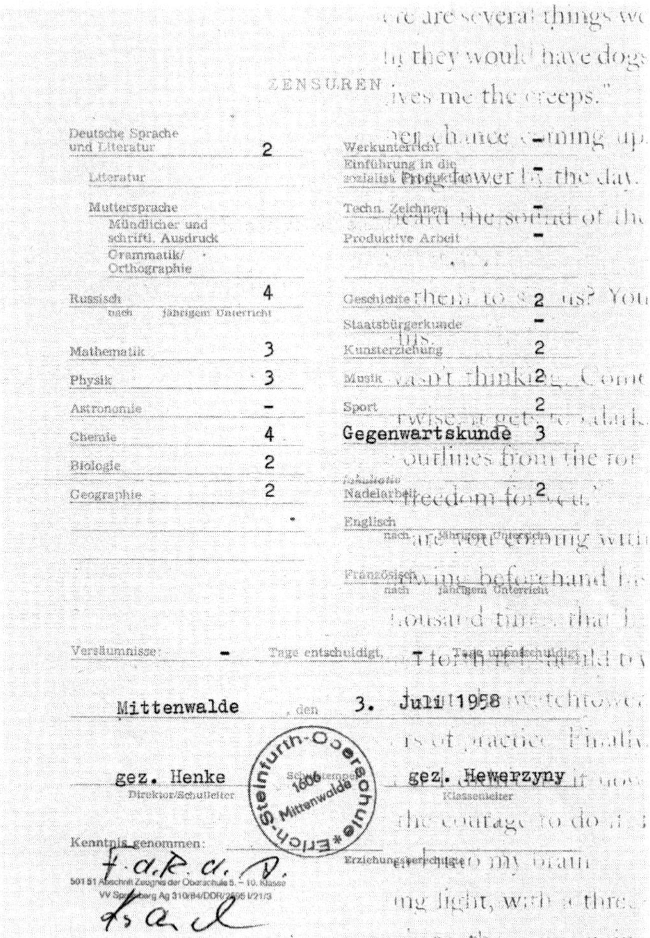

ZENSUREN

Deutsche Sprache und Literatur	2	Werkunterricht	-
Literatur		Einführung in die sozialist. Produktion	-
Muttersprache		Techn. Zeichnen	-
Mündlicher und schriftl. Ausdruck		Produktive Arbeit	-
Grammatik/ Orthographie			
Russisch nach jährigem Unterricht	4	Geschichte	2
		Staatsbürgerkunde	-
Mathematik	3	Kunsterziehung	2
Physik	3	Musik	2
Astronomie	-	Sport	2
Chemie	4	Gegenwartskunde	3
Biologie	2		
Geographie	2	fakultativ Nadelarbeit	2
		Englisch nach jährigem Unterricht	
		Französisch nach jährigem Unterricht	

Versäumnisse: - Tage entschuldigt, - Tage unentschuldigt

Mittenwalde, den 3. Juli 1958

gez. Henke
Direktor/Schulleiter

Schulstempel: Erich-Steinfurth-Oberschule * 1606 Mittenwalde *

gez. Hewerzyny
Klassenleiter

Kenntnis genommen:
Erziehungsberechtigte

f.d.R.d.A.

501 51 Abschnitt Zeugnis der Oberschule 5.–10. Klasse
VV Spremberg Ag 310/84/DDR/2595 I/21/3

Heather wanted me to earn some money as fast as possible. When I was sixteen, Heather had an apprenticeship lined up for me in Königs Wusterhausen. It seemed very important to her having me learn everything to become a salesperson in a grocery store. She told me that I needed to be on the source; this way I knew when deliveries took place and could put items away for the family.

My workday started at 5:00 a.m. During the summer I would ride the bike to Königs Wusterhausen, and in the winter I had to take the train. At first my work consisted of washing out big milk cans, cleaning the store, or filling up shelves. I did not mind it, and it was nice getting to know other people. One evening, several months after I had turned sixteen, I went into a roller coaster of emotions. When I went to the bathroom I discovered my panties bloody and wondered what I had done wrong. Scared stiff to ask anyone about this, I stayed in the train station's bathroom until I reached Mittenwalde. I dared not go home, being afraid of what Heather might do to me, so I hid in the bathroom at the main train station all night. Strangely enough, this place made me think I was sleeping in the basement; it was not much different. The cold and hunger finally made me give up the next morning, and I went home.

Heather did not even ask where I was and why, she just started slapping me around, screaming, "You're just like your mother. You're going to be a whore like her. Not here, not in my house. I don't want to see you anymore." She had already called the juvenile office so they would come to take me away.

When the officers arrived, they were ordered to put me in a home for hard-to-raise children. A very normal thing for a sixteen-year-old girl, such as starting her monthly period, became a turning point in my life. This was the last day I spent in the house at Puschkin Allee. A little suitcase was already packed, and a car was waiting to take me to my new home in Potsdam, about forty minutes from Mittenwalde. I couldn't figure it out; was I angry, sad, shocked, amused, or happy to get away from Heather? In a daze, not looking back, I left Mittenwalde, not to return for a long time.

A NEW SURROUNDING

If my life was limited in freedom before, it became even more limited now. The days were modeled after an army regimen; everything had to happen at a predetermined time. The only difference was that I did not have to get the heaters going in the morning or cook anymore. The three-story house was in a nice area of Potsdam, across from a Russian camp, which was surrounded by a high wall. The doors to the home were opened in the morning and locked at ten at night. The windows had bars but were opened at night for fresh air. There were eight girls in one room, forty in all. The whole house had five bathrooms, with three toilets inside and three outside, which could not be used at night. Two women took care of feeding the girls, two had to see that all were present at night, two made sure that all got up in the morning, and one planned trips for us.

Breakfast was at 6:30 a.m., supper at 7:00 p.m., and lights had to be out at 9:00 p.m. If someone did not show up on time or at all, there was no food available later. A job was found for me in a dry cleaning store, working from 7:00 a.m. to 6:00 p.m. every day except Sunday. The pay was sent to the girls' home, and I received a weekly allowance of five Marks (about $3.50). At work I had to clean out pockets of all kinds of clothing before they were put into the machine to be cleaned. I had to steam the clothes, making them ready for pickup. I was used to hard work and was soon recognized for my good work. I was later placed in charge of the incoming laundry and clothes.

At this point in my life, the new government knocked at my door and made itself heard. Two men, dressed in black, stern faces, and bullying looks, visited our little dry cleaning store every other week. I was ordered into an empty room with three chairs and a table. My knees wobbly, my first thoughts were, *I am going to be arrested,* but that was not on their mind. Instead they told me that I was a good worker and it was time to join the Sozialistische Einheitspartei Deutschlands (Socialistic Unity Party of Germany or SED). Should I reject to do so, I would stay at the same level in my job forever and would have no chances of getting ahead. These visits became regular, and each time I told them that I was not ready for party duties, that I needed to bring my life into order first. I did not know what I wanted, and I was trying to find a way for a better education. After the SED tried about eighteen months, their visits decreased, but did not stop. I wanted to tell them that I liked my work and that I didn't want to do something else right now, but I dared not say this.

My private life went in a lot of different directions. I enjoyed not being afraid of Heather anymore, having time for myself, no cellar with rats, no torture instruments, no beatings, and regular food. I enjoyed the time I had on Sundays, when I did not have to work. I recognized that my fear of everything had started to subside, and I started to venture out more and more; first around the children's home, then around Potsdam. My urge to find out more, to see more and explore grew by the day. My favorite place to visit became the Sans Souci Palace with its beautiful gardens and the interior, which, at this time, was furnished with the original furniture and exhibited the original clothing that the inhabitants had worn. It stunned me every time when I saw how little and small the people must have been at that time, considering their clothing and the small beds.

I still had no real friends, mostly because the bedwetting had not stopped yet, and I was embarrassed about it. The only benefit about it was that no one cared as long as you had your bed made before leaving for work. I continued to work and looked forward to the Sundays. I heard rumors that 2.7 million people had already left East Berlin and that the government was thinking of ways to stop the movement to the West—maybe by requiring written permission or closing the borders altogether.

At work I got to know a colleague, Hans, who did not know about my bed-wetting and who treated me nicely. I liked talking to him, and he liked going to Sans Souci also. We became friends. He would pick me up on Sundays, though never at the girls' home because I did not want him to. Hans had a motorcycle, and I wanted to learn how to drive it. For that, we went to the outskirts of Potsdam. In the country, with no one around, I had the chance to learn how to drive the motorcycle. It was forbidden for Hans to teach me or let me drive the motorcycle, but we did just that when we were alone. Sometimes he would try to kiss me or hold me tight, but I just laughed him off. After a while he stopped and realized that I wanted him as a friend. We got to know each other very well, and I learned for the first time to trust someone. I knew I could tell him about my longing to leave one day to go to the West forever.

July 1960 came and so did my eighteenth birthday. Heather was asked if she would take me back since the girls' home responsibility stopped when the girls turned eighteen. Heather said no. There I was, on July 31, 1960, standing outside the girls' home, with my little suitcase, not knowing where to turn. Hans knew about my dilemma and suggested that I stay with him for a while. I moved in with him and stayed with him for over a year, going to work every day and listening to the ever-growing rumors that a border would be built to stop people from leaving East Germany. Doubts and worries changed to disbelief, and we put it out of our minds. How could they do that; how could they build a border all around East Germany? Lock people up like animals in a cage? No way!

Hans and I had planned a camping trip to a nearby forest for our vacation. I spent two weeks with Hans in a tent. We went dancing, bike riding, fishing, and swimming. Most of the times we talked about the circumstances of maybe being locked in East Germany for good and tried to figure out if the government really could get away with building a border all around East Germany. We drove through the areas where we had heard that there might be a border very soon, now just marked by a little blockhouses.

I had long before made up my mind that if it should

come to such building of a border, I would try to leave beforehand. We talked about my plan, about leaving for good. We discussed a make-believe escape route and how I could realize my plan. Hans became nervous when he realized that I really meant it and really wanted to leave, since he had never thought about leaving. He had always lived in Potsdam, had just seen the area around the city, and was satisfied with it. He was afraid of something new and never wanted to move. My time in Potsdam had changed me; it had revealed another side of me, one that liked adventure and wanted to see and experience new things. I started to make him show me the area along the border close by, bringing his motorcycle as close as possible without making anyone suspicious. When we came closer to a little village, we noticed that there were soldiers, big trucks filled with machinery, and barbed wire was lying on the ground. A newly built watchtower had big flood lights installed, and guards with German shepherd dogs stood around watching the people work. So, all the rumors were true!

They had really started the unbelievable, the unspeakable task of locking in the East German people. I was shocked and became serious about wanting to get out, before it was impossible. Hans agreed to drive with me on the weekends to find a spot where nothing was going on yet, where the crossing was still without guards, watchtowers, and barbed wire. At work our colleagues whispered that almost all East Berlin was locked in already, the border almost finished, and that it was getting harder to get out of East Berlin every day. Even though East German politicians reassured the public over and over again that there never would be a wall between East and West, their reassurance crumbled when on August 13, 1961, the statement came that the German Democratic Republic thought it necessary to build a border to save the ideals of the government, since the capitalistic regime wanted to take over the communist world. The unthinkable happened, but chances to escape still existed. To cut off the whole German Democratic Republic a lot of barbed wire, watchtowers, soldiers, dogs, cement, and manpower was needed. In out-of-the-way places, we still could find areas where borders were not started yet, but this could change in days. We marked the spots where crossing would still be easy, only to see a week later that a hundred-foot gap had been cut into the forest to make room for the border-patrols, watchtowers, mines, barbed wire, and machinery.

After our vacation, we became involved in plans, discussing my possible options, and we bought what was needed for my escape and the first days in the West. We looked, as so many times before, at that precious map I had been given years ago in West Berlin, the map that would one day be my guide to a better life. Maps available in the East part showed only the East; everything in the West part was a white area, a big white zilch. We listened at work closely, when colleagues started quietly talking about the refugee camps, and I overheard one saying that there supposedly was one very close by. We discussed what Hans needed to say after I had left, turning suspicion away from him as a helper. If that could be proven, he surely would end up in jail for helping a fugitive. We set a date and prepared everything. We went with the motorcycle back to the spot once more and saw on the way that it had taken just one week to shut down some of the spots we had marked for crossing. I put clothes in a little backpack, something to drink, a flashlight, a snack, and a little money. We had decided on a spot we knew from the map that could not be very far to the next refugee camp in the west part of Berlin.

THE DREAM OF FREEDOM

OUTSIDE KRAMPNITZ, GERMANY, AUGUST 27, 1961

This is going to be the day. Today I will go through with it, no matter what. We have practiced hours and hours. My little backpack contained only the most necessary things to make it to the refugee camp. I have had to cross about two hundred feet with crawling, hiding, and running. This will decide whether or not freedom or death will prevail…

Hans drove to the crossing point we had decided on. It was outside Krampnitz, a little village north of Potsdam. It was Sunday, August 27, 1961, two weeks since the building of the border between East and West Germany had begun. To our surprise, this spot was already alive with the sounds of machinery digging, soldiers walking with watchdogs, and a watchtower in its final stage of completion.

Hans had parked his motorcycle one mile back so as not to make any noise. We started collecting some brush to hide the motorcycle, not knowing how long it would be until Hans would be back to claim it. We walked the rest of the way and soon after heard the commotion. Hiding behind a small hill, clutching my backpack to my side, we watched what was going on down the hill.

"Come on, Barbara; let's get a little closer," Hans whispered. Crawling closer, he looked at his watch.

"We have about two more hours of daylight for you to look and remember every little detail," Hans whispered. "Are you sure about this, Barbara?" Hans asked again, as he had many times before.

"We've talked about it so many times, and yes, I am not going to miss the life I had here. All the tortures from the woman who called herself my mother; hiding to listen to good music; not being able to read what I would like to read; being without things considered 'luxuries' like chocolates, coffee, nylons, bananas, oranges … well, Hans, you know the list. From my nineteen years in this communist society, I had several close calls from the STASI I'll never forget. Remember when they picked up Ruth's family and put them in jail for *conspiring against the government* and how they approached us because we were five teenagers talking, saying only three people were allowed to accumulate? How about the time they stopped you and took away your radio? You're the one that helped me when my foster mother didn't want me back after I got out of the home for hard-to-raise children."

Hans looked at me with his sad brown eyes. "Okay, okay, we don't have to get started on that again. I know it all, and I understand that your life can only get better than what you had here … but mine is different. I am not going to leave my family here, they need me."

The noise from the machine digging holes for the posts caught our attention again. Sunset started to put the scenery in a mystifying light. The men stopped working, and most went home. Only three of them stayed. One went to the watchtower; the other two stood talking. We could hear them laughing every now and then. Their cigarettes lit up periodically, and after a while, one of the men left. Blue-grayness set in.

"Should I try it? What do you say? We didn't practice a route with barbed wire and it's getting dark. I don't know," I whispered with quivering lips.

"You have to wait for the light to direct you and hit the ground when you come to the barbed wire. It will give you cover until the light is gone and then you have to run." Hans touched me slightly, like he wanted to reassure me that everything would go smoothly.

"I am scared; I don't know. There are several things we haven't prepared for. I never thought they would have dogs here already and the watchtower gives me the creeps."

"Well, you can wait for another chance coming up, but you know these chances are getting fewer by the day." He wanted to light a cigarette; I heard the sound of the lighter, but I hit it out of his hand.

"Are you crazy... do you want them to see us? You know we would end up in jail for this."

"Sorry. I am nervous, too. I wasn't thinking. Come on, I think you have to try it; otherwise, it gets too dark. At least now you can still see some outlines from the forest in the distance... which means freedom for you."

"I'll ask you for the last time—are you coming with me?" I waited for his response, knowing beforehand his answer. He had made it clear a thousand times that he wanted to stay. We debated back and forth if I should try it or not. We were both worried about the watchtower, which was not included in the hours of practice. Finally, I convinced Hans and myself that if I didn't do it now, I would never have the chance or the courage to do it. I watched and carved every little detail into my brain.

The watchtower had a circulating light, with a three-minute interval before coming back to the same point. Every thirty minutes, a soldier passed by with his watchdog, only visible now because he was smoking a cigarette. Watching the soldier, we saw him going to one point—where there must not have been any barbed wire—then crossing the empty area behind it to the other side of the forest edge. That gave us the assurance that they had not had time to install mines in the open field behind the barbed wire yet. After two hours lying in the dirt, we figured out that I had about three minutes to run down the hill and hide; run through the gap in the barbed wire in the next three-minute interval; hide again; and then run across the last fifty feet to safety in the woods on the other side.

We watched the soldier going through that spot between the barbed wire several times. We moved in a little closer and compared the time when the soldier appeared with the time the spotlight came between the barbed wire, and then ended its circle over the open field behind it. We needed to be a lot closer if I wanted to have my full three minutes. The spotlight bathed the area in daylight. I tried, as best as possible, to remember every little detail on my escape route. I knew I had to follow the bright light like ducklings follow their mother duck. I had to run as fast as possible to make it in time to the other side, hoping not to stumble and fall. Hans held my hand and whispered, his voice shaking, "Let's get a little closer, and then you have to do it!" Crawling closer to the edge of the forest, trying not to get hit by the stream of the spotlight, we made it inch by inch as close as it was safe to go. Twigs breaking under us sounded twice as loud. Mosquitoes seemed to think we were the only food in the world, ants crawled on me, and the anxiety made us feel like it was an extremely hot summer day. We got so close that any closer would have been too dangerous. Several times I told Hans, "Bye-bye," and hugged him; then, I backed off, saying, "I'll go the next time."

We promised to write each other, and after three false starts, I took his hand, and he whispered, "Good luck and let me hear from you!"

Adrenaline rushed through my whole body as I focused on what was ahead. Feeling my hands getting sweaty, I waited until the floodlight had hit the edge of the forest and then started running. Stumbling several times, I made it to the gap between the barbed wire, but my pants got hung up in it. Releasing them quickly, I looked around and saw the cigarette light of the soldier about fifty feet from me; I prayed that he did not see or hear me. I hit the ground and got as close as possible to the barbed wire, then waited. The light passed over me, and it stayed quiet. After it came around again, I got up, made it behind the barbed wire, and started running. Suddenly, the dog started barking. As I ran, thoughts sped through my mind about prison cells and being another statistic of a shooting death in a border crossing attempt. Afraid of being shot, I just ran, wondering, *If the light hits me, I'll try to outrun it; running to the left and back to the right would make it hard to hit me.* I lost track of time. The next thing I knew, the light beam was hitting me. I ran to the left, thinking, *Only about fifty more feet,* when I heard several loud bangs and a sound like a baseball zipping by my ear. I realized that it had been gunshots! I was so stunned for a second that I stopped running; I could not think or run. My mind just screamed, *I* want *to make it! I don't want to die!* I kept running, disregarding my shaking knees and the cold sweat. The next thing I remember was falling down, twigs hitting my face, sand in my mouth, and crying, "I don't want to die! I don't want to die!" It took me about ten minutes, still crawling, before I realized no one was shooting anymore. It was quiet and very dark. For all the noise before, it was too quiet now. I looked around and saw the floodlight going nervously back and forth.

The dog started barking again, and the soldier screamed, "Get the light over here. Turn it. Come on!"

The watchtower soldier screamed back, "Okay, okay, take it easy! We will find them."

The light came dangerously close. I was holding my breath when, about three feet from me, it turned away again. Slowly, trying not to make any noise, I kept on crawling and crawling and crawling. Twigs hit my face. Something crawled on me, coming very close to my neck, making me feel terrified. I registered it in my mind but ignored it at the same time.

The sounds of the soldier and the dog barking became more and more faint, giving me unexpected help to crawl in the right direction. I wasn't going to be satisfied until I couldn't hear anything anymore. When I finally sat against a tree, inspecting myself, I realized I was not seriously hurt anywhere. My right ankle was hurting and tears had run down my face without my realizing it. The jeans I had smuggled in years before now had a rip on the knee. Taking off my jacket to get rid of a big bug that had made my jacket his home, I was still nervous, frightened by every little noise. It took a long time until all the tension left, and I allowed myself to get euphoric. Laughing and crying at the same time, I kept on walking for a little while longer until I thought it safe to turn on my flashlight. My light caught an entrance to what looked like a cave. Carefully, I inspected the inside and saw it was suitable for me to get some rest. I collected some brush and put it in front of the entrance, hoping that it was hidden enough. Using my backpack as a pillow, I fell asleep instantly and slept until the light of the new day woke me. It was 11:00 a.m., and I had no idea where I was. I dug through my backpack, found a sandwich and water, and then looked at the crumbled map, trying to figure out where I was. Dirty, longing for a nice hot bath, I tried straightening out my thoughts. I only knew I had made it and that I was free. My heart was full of jubilation and excitement. "I am free, I am free, I am free; I made it, I made it!" I started singing quietly, "Oh what a wonderful morning, oh what a wonderful day." I thought about Hans, wondering if he'd made it home all right. I wondered if he thought I had been killed when he heard the shots and all the commotion. Dear friend, I wished I could let him know that I was all right.

Now I had to find the way to the refugee camp. I followed the sun going west, according to our estimations; I should get closer and closer to a road where I could catch a ride, I thought.

Again, my heart filled with jubilation thinking about the chance I was given for a new life. Excited, I started to jump up and down like a child playing hopscotch. Even though I didn't know what this new life would bring, I was confident that I could handle anything after I had escaped from the lifelong confinement in the East part of Germany.

I must have walked for about two hours, when the sound of cars caught my attention. Sure enough, a street came into sight. Before getting closer, I inspected myself again. My jacket and pants were dirty. I knew my face and hair looked horrible, but that didn't stop me. I had no idea if I should go right or left; I just hoped that someone would stop and ask if I needed a ride. Another hour went by, when finally a car passed by. *A Ford*, I thought. These cars in the West sure looked a lot better than the only two produced in the East—the Borgward and the Trabant.

I had hoped that it would stop, but my demeanor and my dirty-looking clothes must have scared the driver away.

It got quiet for a while again, and I started to get hungry. Suddenly, a voice behind me asked, "Do you need a ride, young lady?" It was an older gentleman with a Mercedes. Wow, I'd never ridden in a beautiful car like this before.

Being as dirty as I was, I looked at him, asking, "Are you sure you want to give me a ride? I am covered in dirt and filth. Won't this destroy your interior?"

"Come on in. Don't worry about my car; I can clean it again. I think it is better if you get off the road. The patrols are always driving up and down this road."

"What do you mean? Am I not in the West part of Berlin? What patrol do you mean? Can they still get me?" I was horrified again.

"Take it easy, young lady. Yes, you are in the West part; the East German patrol still drives along this street, checking for people that look like you. In other words, those who look like escapees." He had a grin on his face. After a while, he assured me he would drop me off at the refugee camp and that everything would be all right.

"I'd like to congratulate you on your successful escape and like to know who am I chauffeuring around."

"Barbara," I told him, wondering if I should have told him a different name. We drove through the outskirts of Berlin. I enjoyed the comfortable ride with my anxiety slowly disappearing. I had a hard time staying awake. I was thankful that the nice gentleman didn't ask a lot of questions. As we came up to the refugee camp, he put one hundred West German Marks into my jacket pocket. "Wow, I haven't seen this kind of money for a while."

I tried to object, but he only said, "You can't get anything with your East German Marks here, so you will need it to start your new life … and good luck."

A last smile, a last "thank you, thank you," and the kind old gentleman drove off in his Mercedes. Hungry and dirty, I stood for a while breathing in the fresh, "free" air. The trees, the houses, the sky, everything looked so much friendlier, and I felt excitement, gratitude, anxiety, and enjoyment all at the same time. Ready for the new life, I walked into the refugee camp ... into a new beginning.

DIAGRAMMATIC DRAWING OF THE BOUNDARY DEFENCES

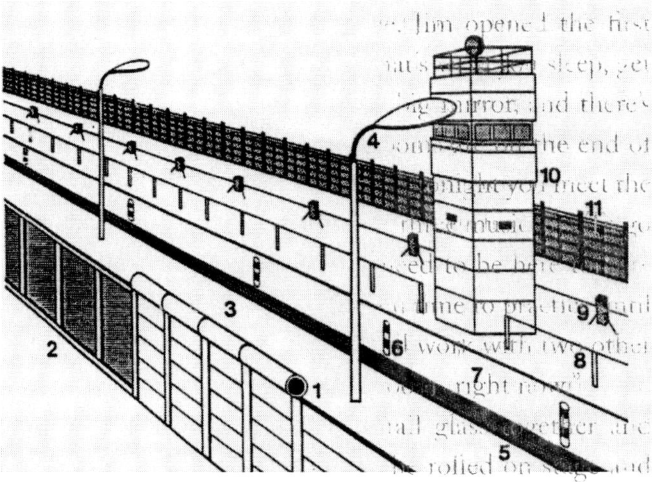

1 Wall of concrete plates with or without pipe
2 Metal meshwork fence
3 Check strip (KS)
4 Floodlighting system
5 Trench
6 Line limiting the farthest outpost of the sentry posts
7 Convoy road
8 Wire for the dog runs
9 Signalling device
10 Watchtower
11 Contact wire

This showed the finished border and its defenses, which would have made it impossible for me to escape.

THE REFUGEE CAMP

I soaked in the sunshine a little bit and looked around me: friendly looking houses with flowerboxes on the window seals; people passing with content, not hardened faces; the smell from freshly baked bread; morning traffic with to me foreign model cars I had rarely seen; children laughing from a backyard somewhere. Exhilarated and with the warm sun on my face, I stood a while enjoying the day. I was ready for whatever lay ahead.

"Auffangslager Marienfelde" (refugee camp) was written on a black board with white paint. I was greeted by an open gate and a sign "Neuankommende zum Haus 24" (New arrivals to building 24). "Barracks" were the first thing that came into my mind looking at the U-form-shaped layout of the exactly alike buildings. A short cold shiver overcame me, but I reminded myself that I am in the West part of Berlin and not in Potsdam anymore where I had seen a layout like this at the Russian camp across the street from the children's home. One building in the middle of the road looked like an administrative building with several office names listed on a big board. All of it gave the impression of hurriedly put together emergency quarters. Most of the buildings were for refugee living accommodations, others for health and dining purposes. The stream of refugees had slowed down considerably since it had gotten more difficult to escape, but the camp was still at about 90 percent occupancy, meaning some people were still in the processing stage that could last up to four months or longer. At the same time others were still finding ways to escape even if it meant risking their lives.

I made my way to building 24 and waited thirty minutes until I was called into a room with a desk and a tired-looking woman behind it. I remember that her desk was a disaster area but had a beautiful Geranium on it and a picture of a smiling blond haired little girl. She pointed to a chair, looked up, and kept on going through her chaos on the desk. "Where are you coming from?"

"Potsdam," I answered.

"Where did you escape from?"

"Outside Krampnitz through the woods."

"Sorry, I am looking for the intake form. I am glad you made it. I bet you are too."

"I still have the noise from the shots in my ears."

"You don't have to worry about that anymore, and you will forget about it soon. Oh, here is the form. Please fill it out and give it back to me. You can use the corner of my desk."

I answered the general questions on the form, when I came to the question, "What problems did you experience that made you want to leave the GDR (German Democratic Republic)?" I thought about it and said, "There is only one line to answer the question. That's not enough. Do you have an extra piece of paper?"

"Just put the most extreme to you on this line. You'll get your chance to name everything later."

I finished filling out the paper, handed it to her, and waited. She looked over it, put it aside, and gave me some papers. In them I got instructions on when to have meals, where I would stay, when to bathe, when I had free time, when to go to which building for hearings, paper completions, or other necessary stamps on forms. With the forms in one hand and my little backpack in the other, I entered my assigned room in building 12, which was located farther down on the left, besides a big poplar tree. Room 7 was in the middle from the entrance and the bathrooms. I entered without knocking and two pair of eyes looked at me suspicious. "Hi, I am Barbara, and I am assigned to your room. Which bed is still free?"

"The bottom one here." A black-haired, petite woman was pointing to it.

"Where are the other ones? I thought there were supposed to be six in the room?"

"They are out getting paperwork done."

"What's your name, and where are you from?" I asked them.

"I am Maria. We lived in Köpenick and escaped in Friedrichhain, swimming through the Spree with my friend Gabi. The darkness helped us, and we were lucky that they didn't have the wires installed in the water yet. It was a weird feeling coming out of the water in the dark and not knowing if we made it and no one to ask. "Where did you come from?"

"I escaped outside of Potsdam, through the forest. They were shooting at me."

"Wow, that's scary. Well, let's talk later. Let's get you settled in and show you around. The others are Czech women and can't speak very much German, but they're nice people; you will meet them later." Maria took over the tour of our building, showed me where the bathrooms and the recreation room were, and told me where we had to go to get food.

I found out later that the other three women had traveled with their husbands the long way from the Tschechoslowakei (later the Czech Republic), pretending to visit relatives in East Berlin, and when there escaping, for 1,000 West Marks each, through a manmade tunnel. Their German was limited, and they showed us by drawings what they had experienced. Their husbands were assigned to the building next to ours.

There I was again, assigned into a room with people who had come from a different part of East Berlin and Communist countries. All were in pursuit of a better life in which they could make their own choices. Living a life without mistrusting each other, travel where they pleased (not just in Eastern Bloc countries), see their relatives in the West whenever they felt like it, and have merchandise available that they had only heard of before.

The room consisted of three bunk beds on each side, a table between them on the wall, a couple of chairs, and a closet. Showers and bathrooms were on the end of a long hall and a separate room had a television and tables for board or card games.

I had put my little belongings in the closet, sat down, and was about to fall asleep. My mind, my body, my emotions, all were still in a chaos, and I had to keep telling myself: *I am all right now. I don't have to be scared anymore, don't have to worry about these horrible two men in black. I can start relaxing and start living without fear.* The future, the past—they needed to be worked out; they needed to be put on hold right now.

Now it was standing in line three to five times a day for food, necessary papers, hearings, and de-fleaing. While standing in one of these lines, I started talking to a young man from Thüringen. It was mostly small talk, and soon he managed somehow to be in the same lines I had to wait in. We had a lot of things in common; he had grown up in an orphanage home, left no connections behind, wanted to be free from the whole Communist system and its restraints. It didn't need long, and we became friends and decided to go to the same town when asked where we wanted to live in West Germany. Rolf was good looking, tall, untamed black hair, brown eyes, and a manly figure. I believed that he knew he was good looking and that he very fast had become my definition of a dream man. When other girls stared after him, he just smiled and said, "But I like you!" He had a brother in Munich who had left the orphanage in Thüringen two years earlier. Otherwise he did not know anything about Munich and neither did I, but we had to give a name of a city we wanted to go to.

Now four weeks in the refugee camp, we had spent our free time going outside the camp, exploring Marienfelde, looking at all the beautiful things offered in the stores or going to the movies. We caught some suspicious looks when standing a long time in front of windows because we couldn't get enough looking at the merchandise displayed, which most of it we had never seen before. The packaging alone caught our eyes in awe, so colorful and inviting. The varieties of food, the way it was arranged, and the abundance of it were hard to comprehend for us who had seen store windows with two or three sausages hanging in it and food items in shelves packaged all in gray, with the name of its content printed on it.

Time in the camp was filled with waiting for a decision or standing in line every day for something else. We kept hearing some horrendous stories from other refugees, hearing about death, hunger, and people fighting insanity having to bury a loved one on the way to freedom. We realized that we were some of the lucky ones who had successfully escaped.

We all had our own demons to fight. After my escape, I still had problems sleeping. Barbed wire stuck to my hair and cloth; a light shining in my face; a gun pointing at me; the barking of a vicious dog beside me; a dark prison cell; my screaming and crying woke me and the others many a times. These nights I stepped outside, sat on the bench under that big poplar tree, and smoked a cigarette, a new soothing habit I had taken on. A lot of nights I got company from others that had also tried to sleep but couldn't. I kept reassuring myself that I don't need to be scared anymore, that I was safe, that I didn't have to look over my shoulder anymore to see who is watching or listening, and that these people in the refugee camp would help all of us to get started with a new life.

After many, many hearings, we were finally considered political refugees. That meant for both of us, with fifteen other refugees, being the first time on an airplane.

A chilly October day brought goodbyes to Marienfelde and the refugee camp. We looked out of the bus windows with mixed feelings, feelings of gratitude, doubt, exhilaration, fear, and anticipation. We headed for a new city, a new beginning and the fact alone that we had to be flown out of Berlin brought back to all the realization of our special status; that of being refugees. The bus ride from Marienfelde to Tempelhof was pleasant and carved a vibrant, beautiful Berlin into our memory. When we passed the Luftbrückendenkmal (hunger fork as the Berliner called it) on the Platz der Luftbrücke in front of the Templehof airport, we were reminded that Berlin had its share of hard times. The statue was erected as memorial for the seventy-eight victims killed during an airlift when Americans flew in and dropped food and other commodities for the Berliners who were blocked off by the Communists from receiving supplies in 1948–49.

The Templehof airport was small but seemed huge to all of us who had never been in an airport. Small shops lined part of the half-round hall; gates were on the end of it, a kiosk with newspapers and flowers in the middle and seating areas splattered here and there. A short last glance at our surrounding, and it was boarding time and getting settled in our seats. We looked at each other and Rolf asked, "Are you afraid?"

I looked away and mumbled, "I am not, but I am. I don't know. Should I be?" I looked at him, and I could tell he was not very relaxed either. I put my hand in his and felt his getting sweaty when the stewardess started talking about emergency air supply, exit doors, and safety precautions. We put our seatbelts on, the engines started to roar angrily and got louder and louder, the airplane started to roll to the starting lane, a short pause there, and the howling engines thrust us into our seats, pressing our hands, closing my eyes, praying, and up, up and away we went—into another new beginning…

MÜNCHEN 1961

A job and a place to sleep were already waiting for me in Munich. Rolf settled in with his brother. A dry cleaning plant had a special house with several rooms for workers without families. One of these rooms became the first room I ever had all for myself. I worked downstairs, lived upstairs. Rolf was assigned a job in an auto shop, fixing cars. On weekends we would go to the movies (I saw my first Hitchock movie, *Psycho,* and was scared all the way home), explore Munich, or just enjoy the freedom of doing anything we wanted to do. For the second time in my life, I experienced what it meant to have someone around whom I could trust and whom I liked to be with. I did not have to worry whether he might turn me in for what I said, and I could talk as I pleased and to whomever I wanted to talk to. It was the end of October in Munich, a big thing, because that meant Oktober Fest, a carnival as big as a city. I never had seen anything like it before, and I was simply fascinated by it: a world of illusions, people everywhere, pushing and shoving, big women (with eight big, stone mugs in their hands filled with beer), polkas, Vienna waltzes, singing, laughing, and screaming. My own happy feelings about my freedom and my new life were expressed in the happy faces, excitement, and celebrations of the crowd around me. A world away from what I faced every morning.

Work started at 7:00 a.m. and ended at 6:00 p.m. One hour was set aside for lunch, which the factory supplied. The day consisted of ten hours working in a circle: one machine pressed the sleeves of a shirt, another one the back, another one the front, another one the collar, and the last one folded the shirt in half. Everything had to go fast; otherwise you might burn the shirts. When one was finished, the next shirt waited already—a regular assembly line. Suffering from the extreme heat and the monotony of it made me start searching for something better.

The weekends, even though Rolf did not want to, pulled me back to the Oktober Fest, and I found myself asking people who worked there if they needed someone. Yes, they always did, I was told. Shortly after that I found myself in a shooting gallery, handing out guns to people and giving out the prizes they won. Watching the people was an experience for me, and I loved it. After I had quit my job in the dry cleaning plant, I was assigned a circus wagon with two beds in it, one for me and one for another girl who worked in a different booth. The bed-wetting still occurred but not as often as before. The circus wagon had no shower, just a washbasin to wash in, and toilets were portable ones supplied by the city of Munich. It did not matter to me because Rolf would come visit me very often. We were in love, and it did not matter where we were as long as we were together. Soon I had to leave him, since the carnival had to make two more stops in other cities before wintertime put a hold on traveling.

Back in Munich for the wintertime, my boss was thinking ahead already, trying to find something for me to do when we could not travel. He sent me to dancing school, which was fine with me. He wanted me to learn how to dance a striptease and travel to make money. Dumb as I was, I thought, *Oh, wow, I love to learn to dance. That's wonderful.* Then I found out what it was he wanted me to learn; I never had heard the word striptease before but found out soon what was involved in learning to dance one. Soon he thought I was ready to leave. I had beautiful new costumes, and adventure was calling. Rolf was not very happy, but he finally agreed to let me go because we calculated on the money I would make to start our life together, and I had promised to write and visit every chance I had.

On February 1, 1962, I had to report to Siegen, close to the French border, for my first assignment. Little did I know that inside of me a new life had already started to develop.

A train trip to Siegen, a short drive with the taxi to a night club, a knock on a door in a busy side street, a sleepy voice answering, and I entered a barely lit room.

"Wait right here; I'll turn the lights on. And by the way, I am Jim. I am sort of the guy for everything. I'll show you around, show you your room, the stage, where the band will be, and everything else."

"I am Barbara, and I'm supposed to dance here for a month." The lights had put a mystical shine on everything, the half-round bar, the big fluffy-looking half-round seat groupings, which all were arranged to face the little stage. Little tables with some of them bottles or glasses on them and full ashtrays were a sign that Jim had not started his cleaning duties yet. Heavy curtains and cheap paintings on the walls, the menagerie of bottles in the shelves at the bar and glasses that hung from frames in the ceiling completed my impression of being in one of the better establishments of nightclubs (Rolf and I had seen worse). The whole club, I estimated, could hold about sixty customers.

"Come on; let's go upstairs to your room so that you can get rid off your luggage." Jim trotted in front of me, looking like he just got out of bed, his thick hair unruly, his clothes wrinkled. Stairs beside the stage led to a hallway with two doors on each side. Jim opened the first one on the right. "That's yours; that's were you sleep, get ready. There's your table with the big mirror, and there's a closet for your costumes. Bathrooms are on the end of the hallway; you start Tuesday night; tonight you meet the owner, the rest of the crew, and the three musicians. To go over your music with them, you need to be here tomorrow around five p.m.; that gives you time to practice until eight p.m. when we are open. You'll work with two other girls, who are asleep in the other rooms right now."

"Who will put my big cocktail glass together and where can it be stored? It has to be rolled on stage and back. I also need warm water in it before the show."

"I usually take care of all this, just show me tomorrow how it has to be." Jim had set down the luggage and had put the costumes on the bed. His big stature turned around, and I saw him clearly for the first time. Warm brown eyes looked me over and with a grin and a gesture of goodbye he left the room. I sat down on the only chair, looked around wondering how many girls had sat down here, nervous and scared as I was right now. I was afraid of how people might perceive me. I was twenty with long, blond hair, and I had a nice figure; I guess you could say I was a pretty woman. My stomach woke me from my thoughts, and I ate the sandwich I had left from the train, unpacked, hung the costumes, checked if they needed mending or ironing, undressed, went to wash up and went to sleep instantly. In the morning I had to think first where I was, which would become a regular thing with all the traveling. The house was still quiet, and I found my way outside into a sunshiny brisk day. I asked a woman for the next bakery and got me some rolls, jam, butter, and instant coffee. The door was still unlocked, and I found my way halfway upstairs again running into Jim. "Where can I make myself a cup of coffee?"

"I forgot to show you the kitchen last night, follow me, and by the way, we eat usually all together. We have a woman coming in to cook every day, but if you want something else, you have to get it yourself." He opened one door leading off the hallway with a big kitchen table in the middle. A stove and refrigerator on one side with L-shaped cabinets and countertops filled with coffee machine, toaster, and coffee cups hanging from hocks under the cabinets. A window put some light in the room. A corner between the stove and the refrigerator had a big cushion on the floor. "What's this for?" I asked Jim.

"That's for 'Night,' our big German shepherd. He's the boss's dog, and he takes him home with him and brings him back with him."

"Does he bite? Where does the boss live? Is he a good boss to you and the others?"

"You have a lot of questions; find out yourself. I got to go clean up. See you later."

I fixed myself coffee and ate and wondered when the other girls would wake up. In my room again, all quiet, I fell asleep again. A knock on the door woke me. "Lunch is ready. Come on and get it." Collecting myself again, I went to the kitchen. A pretty brunette and a red-haired beauty sat on the table with a big woman handing them bowls with food. "Hi, I am Annie, and that's Karla, and that nice lady feeding us every day is Tasha. She's Russian but can understand everything we say but acts sometimes like she doesn't. I think she doesn't like to talk much, but her food is out of this world."

"I am Barbara. Nice to meet you all. How long are you still going to be here?"

"Both of our engagements end on the thirtieth this month, so we'll be together for the whole month. How long are you doing this? We have been wandering from town to town for about two years now, and you?"

"This is my first assignment, and I am very nervous and scared, to say the least."

"We all started some time. Don't worry; we'll help you get through it."

"I need to meet with the band later. What are you going to do until tonight?"

"We need to go and buy some shoes and other stuff; we'll see you before the show."

Tasha had cooked Kassler with potatoes and Sauerkraut. It was delicious and after that, she served vanilla pudding with preserved cherries on top. I thanked her very much and left to get all the stuff I needed for the musicians. Downstairs things were moving around. Jim had cleaned everything, vacuumed, and was busy behind the bar.

"Are you the barkeeper also?" I ask him.

"I told you, I do everything, but I am not alone; I have help in the evenings."

Three men walked in: one smoking and dragging his feet; the other like a panther, quiet and barely touching the floor; the third puffing and snuffing, trying to bring his weight forward. I walked toward them when they came to the bar. "I am Barbara, and I believe you are the band. I have my music with me, and when you ready, we can start practicing."

"Hi, I am Wolf. That's Peter, and that's Günther. Nice to meet you. Let us have something to drink, and then we are ready."

I sat with them on the bar. They had a beer, I had a Coke, and we chatted about this and that, all the time I was trying to hide my nervousness and trying to act as if this was nothing new to me.

After they had settled behind their instruments, they got the notes from me and started playing. Most of the songs they knew and there were only periods I wanted them to put in drum parts. The practice was over, and I had one whole evening to watch Annie and Karla do their thing. Mr. Bauer, the boss, was introduced to me; I was ordered to give my information to Jim and off he went again. The bar had filled up with mostly elderly gentlemen when I went to bed after two shows and two drinks. Sleeping made me forget my nervousness, but it couldn't put the day far away when it was my turn for the stage. The next evening I practiced with the band one more time, and then it was my turn to show my acts. The first was the worst, I messed up several times, but I made it, and the public didn't know how it supposed to be and seemed pleased. I had applause, and Annie and Karla gave me the thumbs-up sign. I put myself in a sort of trance for my next acts, ignoring the audience, getting into the music, and finishing them all without any disasters. I survived the first night and then the second and third…

I earned 100 Marks ($85.00) per night, and soon got over the first month of shyness and shame. Traveling became a normal thing and so did being in one bar after another. When working once with a transvestite, I could not believe the transformation that happened every night, seeing a man going into the dressing room and a woman coming back out. He did a marvelous job of changing into a woman and portraying all the little unique things of a woman. I liked working with him and watched over him. When he had too much to drink, he needed someone to watch that his dress did not slide down and his false breast with it. Another time I came just in time to keep his wig in place before he was to embarrass himself.

A striptease in those times (early 1962) was more dancing than undressing. It was the law that you could only show your breasts for two seconds. My co-worker's bra had a layer of black cloth above the artificial breasts, and when the time came to show his (her) breasts, he (she) just opened that layer, and it looked as if he (she) showed real breasts. Bets were placed, because no one believed that she was a man.

My acts consisted of one number dancing as a prostitute, one as a hula Hawaiian dancer, and the other as a bathing beauty, washing myself in an oversized cocktail glass.

Meanwhile, Rolf came to see me on the weekends, and we made a lot of plans for the future. I earned a lot of money and saved for us, and so did he. But for the time being, it meant traveling from city to city, meeting different people and waiting for the romantic moments we could share together. Not much later I started wondering about my pants getting too tight, my breasts hurting, and not having my monthly period anymore. I wrote my manager about it, and he told me to come to Minden where they were with the carnival, that he would find things to do for me and that he would take care of the contracts that had been signed already. Four months on the road, and my career as a striptease dancer was over. I was not sad about it. He wrote that I was pregnant, which to me was unbelievable since I was told that children came from the cabbage field, and I was far away from our Mittenwalde cabbage fields.

Before traveling to Minden, Rolf came to spend the weekend. I told Rolf about that crazy thing my manager had told me, he looked at me disbelieving, and for the first time I felt scared, realizing that his reaction was not that of a man who was glad about the news he just heard. "What are we going to do?" I asked him.

He waited a while then answered, "I don't know; we don't have anything we can call our own; we don't have a home; we are not ready to have a child. I didn't expect that to happen."

"Neither did I, and I am not ready either, but it happened. We will have a child, and we will be a family, if you want it or not, and we have to figure out what to do next. I did save some money, and if we put our money together, we can rent an apartment shortly before I'll have the baby, get some furniture, and start a family."

"I'll have to think about this; that's just going too fast."

"You will have time to think about it—until the end of July or the beginning of August—that's what I had figured out according to the last time I had my period. Until then I'll have to stay with the carnival to travel because that's the only thing I can do right now. At least I have a bed and work and get fed."

Rolf seemed absentminded, and we parted for the first time without hugs and kisses and promises of writing each other. Our part of the carnival packed up and got ready for travel. Hannover would be our next stay, and we had to travel by train to get there. I had to work in the kitchen to cook for the manager and his wife, clean the wagon, and do other things needed. I also had to learn to be the woman without a head, an illusion shown to the public of the carnival. Mirrors were used to give the public the illusion that I didn't have a head, and when inside the tent, the public was given the impression that the woman without a head had to be fed intravenously. It was shocking to me again and again how people could be fooled and actually believed what they saw, asking ridiculous questions later how a woman without a head could be pregnant, if the baby would be without a head, does the baby get enough food, etc. If they would have waited until the end of our stay, they would have seen the same headless woman climbing the scaffolding of our stand to unscrew screws, unlatch latches, and hand down boards and panels to be put together on a wagon for our next destination.

The letters and visits from Rolf diminished, and I wrote more and more. We came to Hof on the Saale River, and we had three more days in this town when I begged my roommate Hilde to go to the next pharmacy and get me some pain pills. I was hurting very much, ignorant of the fact that I was in labor. Hilde came back after thirty minutes and told me that the pharmacist told her to call the doctor and he didn't give her any pain pills.

"Then call the doctor; I can't stand this pain much longer."

A BABY GIRL

Moaning and groaning, I waited until the taxi finally came to take me to the hospital. One more stop I was told, to pick up the midwife who was barely in the taxi cab when she told me my water had broken. What? What does she mean with this? I didn't care; just get me to the hospital. The taxi squeaked to a hold, I was rolled into the hospital room, a litany of screams followed, and thirty minutes later, I was given a little bundle with the midwife telling me I had a healthy baby girl. *That's what this was all about? Now I am a mother? Where is Rolf? What am I going to do now?* With all these questions in my head, I took a first look at my baby girl. She's beautiful. Black hair, her little fingers and toes, her little nose, I couldn't believe that Rolf and I had created something so beautiful. A shower of love went over me for this new life in my arms, mixed with doubts, worries, and a sense of uncertainty ahead for my sweet baby girl and me. The eight days in the hospital went by, and I was ordered to report to Bamberg, a home for unwed mothers. A train ride with my baby girl and a car was waiting for us to bring us to the home. There I would be able to stay with Gloria until I found a job and an apartment. Another room for myself this time and a clean bed for Gloria in a room with nine other babies, ages from birth to one year old. Five cribs lined each side of the room. Two big windows gave a lot of light and flowers and toys on the window sills made the room a little friendlier. Screaming babies greeted us when I walked in with Gloria in my arms. A nurse was changing a baby who had very short arms and legs. I tried not to be too obvious, showing my shock. The nurse must have seen my questioning look.

"It's diaper changing time, and this is a Contagan baby; we have three more in here. The mothers took Contagan, a sleeping prescription that deformed the babies. They left them here never to show up again. You are lucky that you didn't take that horrible stuff," she said and went on to the next child.

The rhythm of the days set in with me being around Gloria as much as possible, cleaning her, feeding her, and just looking at her. Her dark eyes looked at me questioning; she had a sad look that could melt your heart. Rolf's letters stopped all together, he never came to Bamberg to see his daughter, and I was getting more and more depressed. I found a job at the mental health, mental retardation institution, working in the kitchen and helping out where help was needed. A small place to stay in the institution and meals were included and after my work, I walked to the home to see Gloria. I was in a state of trance, not believing that Rolf could leave me like this, only admitting that he was the father and paying support, but otherwise nothing. I was still writing letters but never got an answer, and one day the letters came back: "Moved, left no forwarding address" stamped on them.

RENEWED HOPE

It was a dreary day in November when a letter for me was left at the children's home. It was from Rolf. Gloria was almost two now, she was still sitting in her crib, sad, and still unable to walk. No one took the time or didn't have the time to potty train her or teach her to walk. The short time I could spend with her was not enough. I visited with Gloria, changed her, and fed her, and all the time the letter was burning in my pocket. I stayed to play for a while with Gloria but cut my visit shorter than usually. I left with the same sad picture as I had seen so many times before and that made me cry inside, searching my brain for a better solution. Gloria's sad eyes, holding her little doll, followed me out of the door, but I couldn't wait to get to my room and read his letter. In my room, I opened the letter and sat down. A one-way ticket to Munich fell out on my lap, and I started reading.

> How are you, and how is Gloria? I am sorry I couldn't visit her yet, but so many things happened. I included a train ticket. Would you please come to Munich because I really need to talk to you. I think I found a way out for you and Gloria…

These lines just swirled around in my head—made me wonder—*Is there hope, and does this mean that there is a chance for Gloria and me? Maybe he's talking about marriage and a home?* A home—the word alone produced warmth. How wonderful the thought and the sound. I started dreaming, imagining, and seeing a two-bedroom apartment, maybe a balcony and a nice area of Munich where Gloria would have other children to play with. One more week and I would see Rolf again, and maybe my future had the role as a wife and mother in it.

I had asked for a two-week vacation, told the children's home, and was wished good luck by the nurse who usually took care of Gloria. I had bought a new dress, got my hair done, everything to look good for Rolf. My little suitcase was packed and a last visit with my sad-eyed Gloria telling her that I would be back soon to get her and start a new life in a home with her daddy and mom together.

The ride to the train station was short, and the rainy and chilly weather couldn't crush my spirits, knowing I would see Rolf in four hours. I found my compartment, settled down, and hoped that with my anxiety growing I could convince the train to go faster and faster. Finally, the train rolled into the Munich Main Train Station. It was four thirty in the afternoon, and darkness started to set in. My eyes searched for Rolf, but I had to wait until we all came out of the gate, and there he was. Handsome as always, he walked toward me with a walk like a panther, smooth and confident, and then we stood in front of each other.

"Hi," he said and did no move to hug me or hold me, kiss me, nothing.

"Hi," I said, and my heart sunk to my feet. I couldn't walk and was unable to look at him. "I need to sit down a minute," was all I could say. I know in this instant that my visit here was not going to be what I expected. He took my suitcase and directed me to one of the little cafés; we set down, ordered, and were quiet for a while. Rolf looked at me.

"You are pretty as always. How are you doing? How is Gloria? Is she big and as pretty as her mom? Every time I wanted to come and visit, something came up. I am now a supervisor in a large company that makes parts for automobiles. What are you doing?"

"I work in a mental health, mental retardation home, and I like it. Gloria is a very sad little girl who still can't walk and is still not potty trained."

"She's over two; shouldn't she be able to walk and use the bathroom by herself? Do you have a picture of her?"

"The people in the home do what they can with all the children they have and not enough staff." I got a picture out of my wallet and showed it to Rolf.

"She looks like me; I can't believe it. That's crazy. But she's a pretty little girl. Too bad I couldn't see her, but I also think its too late now. She wouldn't know who I am."

"I did show her your picture a lot of times, but that's not the same, and I told her about you too."

"What did you tell her? That I don't want to see her? That's not true you know, but my work was eating me up. I really had to do a lot to get to be supervisor, you know. Let me bring you to the hotel I reserved a room at, and tomorrow we can get together and talk."

Before I knew it, we were in a taxi and on the way to the hotel. "A hotel. I thought I would stay with you when I am here?"

"No, but we'll talk about everything in the morning.

I'll pick you up at ten in the morning, we'll go somewhere where we can have peace and quiet, and we'll talk, okay?"

"I guess I don't have any choice in the matter, do I?"

"I just think you are tired right now, and we need a clear head for what we have to discuss. See you tomorrow morning. Good night, Barbara."

A room key was shuffled into my hand, a boy grabbed my suitcase, and I was led to a room on the second floor in the, in my opinion, too fancy hotel. Entering, my eyes noticed a nice big bed, a separate bathroom, a TV, an alarm clock, a table with two chairs, a closet, and heavy gold trimmed curtains, which completed my inspection of the room. After the hotel boy had left, I sat on the bed and replayed what just happened, from the train station to the hotel room. Everything was not good, not good at all, and I realized that I was wishing and hoping too much and that reality would look a lot different than what I expected. My anxiety finally let go, and I went to sleep telling my restless mind that tomorrow I would find out what it all meant.

The rain hitting the window woke me. I, first, had to figure out where I was, and I rubbed my eyes thinking I was dreaming, but then the memory came back. I was in Munich and would soon see Rolf again to find out what my visit here meant. I showered, told myself, *Why not enjoy a little luxury as long as I can?* and ordered breakfast. Rolf would come to the room, and hope was still lingering in me that we would have a future together despite his strange behavior yesterday. I put a lot of effort in how I looked; I wanted to look my best for him. I listened to my heart when I asked myself if I still loved him, and it said yes. I couldn't help it, he was the father of my child, and we had been through so much. I searched my brain, remembering all the things he loved so much; I wanted to do everything to get him back from wherever he was. He belonged to me and to no one else; we had shared first love, refugee camp, and explored capitalism and a new life together. He followed me when I was on the road to renew our love and to plan for the future. For years we never doubted that we would spend the future together, and I didn't want to believe that this had changed. I was looking at the rain, sitting in a comfortable chair; I must have dozed off again when a loud knock on the door woke me. A quick look in the mirror, and I opened the door. Rolf came in, handsome as always. "Did you sleep all right?" he asked with a grin on his face.

"Yeah, matter of fact; I slept like a princess, thanks for the room and everything."

"You look beautiful. Do you want some more coffee or something before we get serious? I'll order something to drink for me."

"Yeah, I'll take more coffee. What do you mean getting serious?"

"Just a minute, let me order first," and he went to the phone and placed our order.

"You look and smell so good, I have to hold back not to rape you." I tried to take the tension out of the air.

He laughed. "You still like my cologne and still like me, ha?"

"Not like you, still love you and I surely would like to know why you stopped writing and never came to see your daughter. What did I do that was so bad? What did your daughter do that was so wrong?"

"Hold it, hold it. Let me explain. You both didn't do

anything bad or wrong. It's me that did all the wrong things. Let's go back to before you had Gloria. I had changed jobs, had started with this company I am still with today. I worked myself up to supervisor, but that had meant long hours, overtime, and sometimes no weekends."

A knock on the door, and a waiter brought in our order. I filled my coffee cup again and wanted to know: "So you use your new job as an excuse why you never wrote and came to see us?"

"No, Barbara, there is no excuse, I know; but listen. After I worked for the company about eighteen month, the boss came one day and introduced me to his daughter. Katrina had just finished her studies at the university and started to work at the company she would one day have to take over from her parents. She loves all the things that have to do with it and has learned everything to advance it into the future. At first, she came by my work place; she asked questions, said "hi," and that was it. Then we had our yearly Christmas party where we suddenly found ourselves dancing together and sitting together at one table, engulfed in serious conversations about everything. I found out that she was raised a strict Catholic and that she believes that people shouldn't get married if the man has fathered a child and has to pay alimony. I don't agree with it, but that's the way she felt, and I came to the conclusion never to tell her about you and Gloria. Needless to say, I am deeply in love with her and want to marry her. We have so much in common, and I don't want to hurt her telling her, and I don't want to lose her either. So here is what I thought of, and please think about it before you answer. I don't want an answer today; I am willing to wait for a month or two. I hope you don't explode right away when I tell you—well, what do you think about having Gloria adopted? This way she would have a family, and as I found out, this family wouldn't get her unless they are financially well off. Think what her future would look like otherwise, always in a home. Maybe you'll get married one day, but when will this be? She needs love from both a mother and father and a stable home. Also, this would mean I don't have to pay alimony anymore, and Katrina never needed to find out about it. I know it sounds selfish at first, but think about it, and please think about Gloria and if you are really doing her a favor by hanging on to her when your future is so uncertain. Like I said, that's something you need to think about, and I'll wait for your answer."

The room stayed very quiet for a while. I was stunned and couldn't comprehend the meaning of it all right away.

"You sure asking a lot, and there I thought I would come here to hear a marriage proposal and that we would finally be a family. I am sorry, I am really disappointed right now, and I think you'd better leave. I have to be alone; I can't think straight with you around."

"I am sorry, I know I am asking a lot, but I wanted to suggest this in front of you and not in a letter. Think about it, please; think about Gloria, and I wait to hear from you." He got up, turned around, and was out of the door.

I don't know how many hours went by. I cried, cursed, calmed down, and finally came to a decision. I would stay in Munich and would try to win Rolf back, make him change his mind, and convince him that I was the right woman for him. Checkout time was getting close, and I had to make another decision: where to stay here in Munich, surely not in this hotel. I got a telephone book and tried to remember who, from people I used to know, still lived in Munich. I found three friends that still had the same telephone number. The first one I called had gotten married and had a child. I congratulated her, told her we have to get together one day, and hung up. The second one had already two roommates and no room to spare. The last one I asked if I could stay a while until I get my own place said yes and told me to come to the house right away since she had to go to work soon. I checked out of the hotel, got on the subway and on the street car, and shortly afterward rang a doorbell at a four-story house.

"Hi, Barbara. Come on in and have a seat, and I'll bring us coffee. You want some, don't you?" Helga went into the next room from which the sounds of water running and dishes being shuffled around came. It seemed to be the living room in which I was, with a sofa bed still open, cloth laying around, and a cat sleeping on the windowsill. "So, how did you know my telephone number?" she asked, coming back with a tablet full of coffee and cups and cookies.

"A friend I had met in Bamberg had given me your number—Conny. Do you remember her?"

"Oh yeah, I remember, she didn't stay with me very long. How is she doing? She was a nice roommate; too bad she had to leave."

"She's doing fine; she got engaged last year and wants to get married in May. Her fiancé is also very nice and has a terrific job; they don't have to worry about money."

"That's nice; do you want to see the room I have for you? Come on, this way." And she led me through a hallway into a room in the back. "The bathroom is in the hallway, you can use the kitchen, and the only thing I ask is that you clean up after yourself. I ask 200 Marks on every first of the month. There is a German shrank, a table with two chairs, and your bed. Do you want it?"

"I'll take it" was my reply, and I asked her if I could stay right away. She was fine with it, and I was happy to have a place to stay.

...ething bad happened?
... out of the apartment?
...b? Tell me."
... have time to sit down

...ous to find out what
...se over for a while; my

...lleague and came back
... pastry for both of us.
...econd; tell me what's

...had happened, and after
... me stunned. Quietly
... bite from the pastry.
...o Berlin to find out."
...r lack of funds for such
...e would find a way for
... advance, and you can
... enough for the train
...here you could stay for a
...ut. You know your way
...h to ask your boss for
...n, call that lady to find
... knock on her door."
... don't know if I'll have
... know what to say ...
... shut the door on me,
...

...u won't find out, will
...ed to know, otherwise,
...ways wondering if you

KEEP ON LIVING

In trance—that's the only way I could describe the time that followed. Tears, doubts, numbness, disbelief, and resistance to go on changed daily, but I had to let the home in Bamberg know that I would have to work in Munich for a while to get the money together for a trip back. The job search took my mind of my misery for a while, but the realization of what qualifications I had was very depressing, leaving me with the only option of going back to the dry cleaning business or what? I finally found a job in a bar as waitress—that couldn't be too hard to do. Helga told me that she would let me know if there is something available in the shopping center she worked at. She became my friend in this time of indecisiveness when I often cried on her shoulder; she gave me strength and good suggestions concerning Gloria. Her visions of Gloria's life in the future put chills up my spine, but she told it like it was. When would I be able to give Gloria a home and be able to care for her? I knew she was right and without support from anyone I knew myself that it would be very selfish putting a child in this uncertainty. I would need room, a person to take care of Gloria when I worked, and most of all a job that would make a lot of money to afford this. The money Rolf paid to the home in Bamberg would stop, and that's what he wanted. Helga and I debated Gloria's future often, and the fact that Rolf called again and again if I had made up my mind about Gloria, that he wanted to get married and wanted her adopted before didn't help me to come to a decision.

Another visit to Bamberg finally brought the assurance for me that Gloria would definitely be better of in a family, out of that home. My visit was a surprise one, and I walked right into the room where I last saw Gloria. I had some cookies in my hand from the train trip. It was a long time since I had seen Gloria, but it seemed like time had stood still in this room. She was lying in a play pan on a plastic mat and a bad smell was around her. When I called her name, she looked up but didn't move. She just looked at me with these sad eyes that focused on the cookies in my hand and slowly got on her knees, crawling to the edge of the play pan. It seemed that the cookies had become the driving force for her crawling. One of the nurses came in: "You should have called before; you just can't wander in here."

"I wanted to see how a regular day is for Gloria and couldn't wait to see her," I told her. She was a nurse I hadn't seen before, and I instructed her to bring me some water and towels so that I could clean Gloria and pick her up.

"You can get it yourself; all you need is just around the corner."

"When was the last time Gloria got something to eat?" I asked her.

"I don't know; I have to ask the other nurse." She turned and left the room.

I got some water and towels, looked in the drawers

for some clean cloths for her, and started to clean her and the mattress. I couldn't believe that she still was wearing a diaper that seemed to have been changed days ago. Gloria just looked at me; she didn't seem to care and surely didn't recognize me. I had put her clean cloth on when Mother Gertrud came walking in. "So you made it finally to visit your daughter again?! What kept you away so long?" she asked and looked at me with her cold eyes.

"Good day, Mother Gertrud. Life didn't let me come earlier; I needed money for the trip. My future of being a married mother didn't work out as I thought when traveling to Munich. Gloria's father decided to marry someone else and wants Gloria adopted so he doesn't have to pay for her anymore and doesn't have to tell his very Catholic future wife about her."

Mother Gertrud looked at me, telling me that it's maybe better for Gloria being adopted than living in this home without a father and a mother.

"That's the decision I came to also, and my visit here destroyed the last doubts I had. I'll call Gloria's father when back in Munich. He has the papers ready for quite some time, and I'll sign them to get the adoption started."

"I think that's a good decision, considering Gloria's future, not yours. She needs loving parents, a home, and stability. I guess I'll get some paperwork in a while. Take care of yourself." And that's the last time I saw Mother Gertrud.

I spent two days in Bamberg with Gloria trying to teach her how to walk, put her on the toilet, changed her diapers, fed her, and talked to her. I explained to her the circumstances, all about her father and me, that she hopefully would get a good home and a lot of love she deserves. That I wouldn't see her anymore since that was the law; that she would always be in my mind, and that we might meet again after she turned eighteen if she wanted to see me again then. The second day was torture—Gloria must have sensed something; she was very cranky, cried, and was not pleased with anything I did. I picked her up, and we cried together. I felt her little arms around my neck squeezing me a little, but then she wanted to push me away. *Did she understand everything I told her?* I ask myself. I wished with all my heart that she understand that it was for her own good. That she needed to get out of a situation without a future. That only good will happen to her and she gets a chance of life. I kept telling it to myself over and over, but it didn't do much good right now. Holding my child for the last time for many, many years, having to let go, it broke my heart. The evening came, one more hug and kiss combined with tears, one more time to say goodbye, one more attempt to sketch a picture of Gloria into my mind. A last look. A last, "Goodbye my sweet and sad Gloria. I'll think about you all the time and hope that your life will be full of love."

I couldn't see the streets clearly on my way to the train station. After I found my compartment, I put my bag in the overhead place and went to the bathroom to clean up, but the tears kept coming. The other people in the compartment didn't ask any questions, and I was glad about it. I finally dozed off and woke at the "Munich Main Train Station" announcement. The streetcar brought me the rest of the way, and I sneaked into our apartment not to wake Helga.

The next day I called Rolf and told him about Gloria

and my decision to find her new parents. I told him how I found her in the home, neglected, unable to walk yet, dirty, hungry, and not potty trained yet. He was glad that I had come to the decision and reassured me that it would benefit Gloria. He would send me the papers to sign, and he would take care of everything that needed to be taken care of from here on. "Good luck, Barbara, and if you ever need something, let me know," and he hung up. I felt like the last remnants of the story of Rolf, Gloria, and I suddenly dissolved. Erased—didn't exist—nothing left over, except in the minds of a handful of people.

Helga became my support, my psychiatrist, my conscience, my drive to live from one day to another. She pushed me when I thought I didn't have the strength, she told me like it was when I did something stupid, and she cried with me when it was necessary. I started working again and all the time looked for something better…

ula came to my seat, and
her half-sisters. Wow, I
e have the same mother.
it my arms around the
nting their tears.
ister, someone I knew
mily. I can't believe it
what I was looking for
real breath of destiny

ee us some coffee, and
ne to her two children
p of trouble. And that
sweetheart."
my lap and hugged me.
a bring me a toy?" He
angle, and he was down
unses

your room. She'll bring
ay?" Brian looked at me
ared into the next room.
eth; bring me a robot."

ing right now." Ursula
e quiet for a while, or

minute, so I can get us
alked out, and I sat
my lap, looking at me
ng her wet finger in my
put it in my eyes. I p

A BREATH OF DESTINY

MÜNCHEN, GERMANY, 1964

The subway moaned and groaned as it made its way through the blue-gray tunnels of Munich, Germany. It was the wee hour of the morning, and people huddled in their seats, some even using their neighbor's shoulder to get in another wink of sleep before the demands of the day forced their attention. Squeaking, the subway came to a halt. "Leopold Platz," the speaker blared. That was my stop. I hated the German law that made people report their new addresses, and I dreaded all the bothersome steps, considering it all unnecessary German bureaucracy.

I was greeted by rain when I came out of the subway station. Fitting my mood, the streets and buildings had put on their coat of dreariness, and store windows seemed to look at me with prying eyes. Walking, I thought again about that reoccurring dream that had followed me since I could remember—a little girl in a main train station with her parents and an older sister. A swarm of people was coming toward them, pushing and shoving, separating her from her sister's hand and shoving her into the train. Crying and screaming, "Mom, Mom, help. Dad, no please, help, don't let me go!" The train started moving, and she couldn't get out of it. My imagination ran wild with me a million times when thinking about this dream. I imagined a loving father and mother, and I so much wanted a sister to play with. I had grown up with a foster mother and no siblings, only the neighbors' children and a cat to play with. My longings for companionship grew even stronger over the years. Except for Hans and Rolf, I had been by myself since I was sixteen, and some of the jobs I had taken were not my idea of making a living, but I had done them in order to survive.

The rain had enveloped my whole being, and walking into the police station, I never would have thought that a dreary day like this would change my whole life.

Twenty-six, brunette, and of medium size, I had been told that I was good looking. Munich had become my first city to live in after the escape from East Germany. Though Munich had not held me for very long, but after traveling and living in Hamburg, Siegen, Bremerhaven, Koblenz, Hannover, Frankfurt, Bielefeld, and Wiesbaden, I had come, three months before, back to Munich. Life itself pushed me, usually after eighteen months, to move on to the next city. There it would start again, that overwhelming urge to move again, hoping to find in the new city that feeling of belonging, find a family, or find someone I could belong to.

It was late September, and Leopold Strasse was always full of people who tried to get home or do some last-minute shopping. Most of them pushed toward Woolworth or the other big shopping centers to get bargains for the upcoming holidays. I had lived in München (Munich) altogether four years now and still had a hard time getting used to the shoving and pushing at rush hour. I had moved to the west part of Munich, sharing an apartment with my best friend Helga. Helga and I, we were always there for each other; we had experienced hard times and good times together. When I first moved to Munich, we were living in separate apartments until moving together after my last return. We had a lot in common, such as being the same age, no parents, no home, and nowhere to go. Helga worked during the day as a waitress in one of the big shopping centers downtown. All the restaurants in the shopping centers were on the top floor. I worked late in the evening until the morning hours in one of the more exclusive night clubs downtown, which stayed open all night, and I seldom came home before Helga had to leave for work. We enjoyed our Sundays together, going to the movies, sitting outside on the veranda in Biergartens watching people go by, and talking about our dreams, hopes, and the future. When I had a weekday off, I would spend time with Helga in the restaurant and going shopping afterwards. The "Wiesen," a huge empty field where every year the Oktoberfest took place, was just five minutes away from our apartment and a place the people enjoyed going to every year during late October and the beginning of November.

Now, I had to hurry to make it to the police station in time to get my Ausweiss (similar to a driver's license ID) renewed. I had taken off one day from work and didn't look forward waiting in line, getting my picture taken, and being interrogated about my moving from one city to the next. I was lucky, having to wait only thirty minutes until I could approach a man behind the window. A middle-aged, gray-haired man looked up at me with questioning hazel eyes. "What can I do for you?"

"I need my Ausweiss renewed and my address

changed." I handed my documents through the bottom open part of the window.

"I see you moved a long time ago, why did you waited so long to report this?" he asked.

"I thought I'd do it all together, saving you and me time," I answered, putting my best smile on. I hated the German bureaucracy and still couldn't figure out why it was necessary to report where I lived.

The man behind the window looked at me puzzled. He looked at me again and again and finally told me. "That's too weird, I moved to Munich about three months ago and I have worked in Berlin before. Your last name is not a very common name, and I definitely remember this name. I issued an Ausweiss where the maiden name was the same as yours in Berlin about four months ago to an Ursula. Is this a relative of yours?"

"I don't know. I don't know of any sister and never heard anything about other siblings, but I guess anything is possible." My dream popped into my mind again, and I asked the man, "Would you consider giving me the address for this Ursula in Berlin?" The thought crossed my mind that there maybe was some benefit in it making people report where they live.

"Well, I am not supposed to, but I think this is worth further investigation. Okay," he said after a while, "and I surely would be interested to find out if you two are sisters. Let me know the next time you come, will you?"

I took the address, still puzzled, and promised to let the man know the minute I found out. Walking back to the subway my thoughts raced in all kinds of directions. Was the dream reality, was I really a lost child, did I had loving parents and a sister? Maybe my parents were rich, and I wouldn't have to work anymore. Maybe my parents and sister were looking for me. Maybe Barbara wasn't even my real name, but how come the last name was the same? How come they couldn't find me? My head started spinning, and I knew I needed to talk to someone. Outside again, I took a deep breath, went to the subway station, and took the escalator down to it. Automatically, I turned to the subway that would bring me to Leopold Strasse and to Helga. Deep in thought, I didn't see or hear anything. The immensity and importance of this incident still was trying to sink in.

"Leopold Strasse," I heard the loudspeaker announce when the subway rolled into the station. I woke up from my daydreaming and jumped up to get out. These thoughts still kept racing through my mind, creating all sorts of fairytale endings. I walked faster and faster to get to Helga who, I knew, would help me to sort out this mystery and help me to make a decision. In my mind I tried to figure out if I could afford a trip to Berlin, if I could take off from work for a week, or if I even should go. The elevator finally stopped at the top floor, and I started to look for Helga. Her long black hair and her petite figure made her easy to find, as she was helping a customer who was paying his bill. I looked for a table in Helga's section and waited for her. Helga had still to serve several customers before she came to my table asking, "What can I bring you?" Looking up, Helga laughed and said, "Oops, I was thinking about something else and didn't realize it was you. What's going on? How come you're here at this time?"

"I need to talk to you desperately, and it cannot wait until you get home," I responded.

"Wow, you sound serious. Something bad happened? Did they raise the rent or throw us out of the apartment? Are you sick? Did you lose your job? Tell me."

"Hold it, wait a minute, do you have time to sit down a while so I can tell you?"

"I'll make time, I am too curious to find out what's going on. Let me tell Brenda to take over for a while; my break is coming up anyway."

Helga went to talk to her colleague and came back with something to drink and some pastry for both of us.

"Now, I can't wait another second; tell me what's going on," she said.

I told Helga everything that had happened, and after I was finished, Helga looked at me stunned. Quietly Helga sipped on her coffee, took a bite from the pastry, and finally said, "You have to go to Berlin to find out."

I tried to argue, mentioning our lack of funds for such a trip, hoping nevertheless that we would find a way for me to go. "I can ask my boss for an advance, and you can do the same. That should give you enough for the train ride. I know someone in Berlin where you could stay for a couple of days to check this story out. You know your way around Berlin, so get going to work to ask your boss for an advance. When you get to Berlin, call that lady to find out if she's at home, and then just knock on her door."

"You make it sound so easy. I don't know if I'll have the guts to just go there. I don't know what to say to her, and I am afraid that she'll just shut the door on me, thinking I am some kind of lunatic."

"Well, if you stay in Munich, you won't find out, will you? I want to know, and you need to know; otherwise, you'll never be the same again, always wondering if you have a sister or not. So, don't tell me you don't have the spunk; I know you do."

Helga sat for a while with me, but then she had to go back to work. I left, promising to ask my boss about an advance and a week off.

The weekend was coming up, and it was decided that I would take a Sunday night train with a sleeping compartment for the eight-hour ride. A little suitcase was holding my most necessary belongings, which I put in the overhead place. I had the compartment all to myself. I cleaned up in the bathroom adjacent to the compartment and got ready for bed. A knock on the door, the conductor wanted to see my ticket, and then I was ready to get comfortable in the bottom bed. Lying there, I tried to clear my mind and let go of all these thoughts, and tried to listen to the monotonous noises of the train, which slowly put me to sleep. I didn't know how long I had been sleeping when a knock on the door woke me again. "Ausweiss Kontrolle" (passport check) a voice said outside my door. East German patrollers had boarded the train to check passports. I had to travel approximately four hours through East German territory, and this was a common procedure when traveling to West Berlin. I handed the guard my passport with an uneasy feeling, thinking back to the time I had escaped from East Berlin. The guard looked at my pass, looked at me to see the resemblance on the picture, mumbled, "Thank you," and left. I went back to sleep, waking to the sounds of the conductor announcing the arrival in Berlin in twenty minutes. Still sleepy, I looked around and had to remember where I was and why. I refreshed myself, grabbed my little suitcase, and realized suddenly how hungry I was. "Berlin Main Train

Station" sounded the speaker. A busy beehive, that's what it reminded me of. Everywhere people, even this early in the morning. A musician playing his guitar, vendors were trying to sell jewelry, and a kiosk sold the latest news. I picked a restaurant to have breakfast, ate, and looked for a telephone. I called the telephone number where I was supposed to stay for a couple of days.

"Who's this?" a sleepy voice answered the ringing.

"Sorry, didn't mean to wake you. This is Barbara from Munich. I am supposed to stay with you for a couple of days. Is it all right to come?"

"Oh, yeah, yeah, I just need to wake up. Just grab a taxi and come on over. See you in a little bit," the voice answered.

I stepped outside to an awakening city, wondering what news I would have when arriving at the train station again, a couple days later, to go back to Munich. A long line of taxi cabs awaited customers. I took one, told the driver the Wilmersdorfer address thinking that this woman, who maybe was my sister, lived in this section of Berlin as well. Wilmersdorf was one of Berlin's better parts to live in. Looking out of the window, I saw big apartment houses everywhere, usually with all kinds of stores on the bottom floor. In my memory I saw parks flashing by, the Siegelsäule (victory column); the Brandenburger Tor; Peacock Island with the pretty castle; all the wonderful castles and museums and other beautiful points of interest in this beautiful city.

Restaurants started to get ready for another business day. A waiter stepped outside looking at the sky and started to put tablecloths on tables. Not much had changed in Berlin, I thought, but now Berlin might change my whole life.

The girl I would stay with opened the apartment door, still looking sleepy and half-dressed. Her brown eyes looked at me from head to toe and a hoarse voice murmured, "Come on in. So you are the girl in search of a sister, huh?"

"That's me all right. Barbara is my name. What's yours?"

"Wanda, come in; I'll show you where you can sleep. There are three of us, one just left to get married in Hamburg, and all of us work at different times, so don't be disturbed when the door opens in the middle of the night or early in the morning. How's Helga doing? I liked her and was sad when she moved to Munich."

"She's fine and working; she says hello and you should write sometimes."

"I will, but now I've got to get ready, I need to be at work in one hour. Make yourself comfortable. Oh, by the way, help yourself to what's in the refrigerator, you can cook yourself some coffee and the telephone book is on the shelf in the kitchen above the telephone. I know you need it to call ahead. Good luck with the visit. Hope it is what you expected." Wanda left the room, and I was by myself. I looked around the room, sat on the bed, and tried to get my thoughts together on what to do next. A little table, a chair, a closet, a dresser with a radio and a little lamp on it, and the bed were all different furniture styles. They all looked like they had a lot of stories to tell. Two pictures showed reproductions of Monet's *Waterlilies* and Von Gogh's *Cornfields*. The sun started to creep into the room, putting it all in a friendly, cheerful light. I put water in the shiny teakettle and put it on the stove. I heard the door close, meaning Wanda had left for work.

Biting into a slice of toast, I put the telephone book on the table and looked for Ursula's address and telephone number. There were three listings with the same last name, but only one with the right address. I stared at the sunlit window for a while and then, a little shaky, dialed the number hoping that this Ursula was at home.

"Hello, who's this?" an anxious voice answered. I was too nervous to start talking right away, and the voice asked, "Well, say something. I have a crying child in the next room that needs attention."

"Hi, my name is Barbara. I was wondering if I could come to visit with you. I need to ask you some questions."

"Barbara Krämer you said?" A long pause and then, "What was your first name again?"

"Barbara, could we meet somewhere to talk?"

"That's not a good idea; I need to stay here with my children. Can you come to my place?"

"Yes, I can. Would it be okay to come in an hour or so?" Another long pause followed. I sat back in the chair, looked at the clock, and thought about children. *She has children. I wonder how many and if her husband would be there too.*

"Yeah, okay, I'll see you then. Oh, I hope you know how to get here or just take a taxi—I assume you have my address?"

"Yes, I see you then." I got up, in a monotonous, numb way went to the bathroom to take a shower and wash my hair. I didn't know what to expect and what kind of reaction I would have if this woman was my sister. I put on a skirt and the maroon sweater I liked so much, looked at the clock again, took the key for the apartment, and locked the door after me. I remembered a taxi stand around the corner where one of them stood waiting.

I told the driver the address; he looked at me, saying, "Lady, you could walk, Luisen Strasse is just around the corner. You still want me to bring you there?" I was embarrassed.

"Sorry, I haven't been in Berlin for a long time. I've forgotten, and I am too nervous to walk. I need to sit down."

I got out of the taxicab and gave the driver a good tip, which put a smile on his face. I stood before a red brick building four stories high. I could tell this building had seen some rough times with its bullet holes on the walls and places that looked charred from fire. I had forgotten to ask which floor Ursula lived on, and the nameplates didn't say. I opened the heavy wooden entrance door and started looking at all the names on the doors. On the second floor I found P. Wending. Ursula's married name. Taking a deep breath, I put my finger on the doorbell, but didn't push it. Doubts grabbed me again, but I told myself 'I have to know' and rang the doorbell. A little while of quietness, then the door swung open and a young woman with a little girl in her arm opened the door.

"Hi, I am Barbara. I was wondering—was your mother's name Greta and was her birth date July 22, 1919?"

Ursula looked at me puzzled with her blue eyes, told me to come inside so she could look at me closely. She closed the door behind her and led me to a living room. She looked at me again, told me to sit down and said, "Yes, my mother's name is Greta, and that is her birth date. My father's name is Erwin."

A long pause followed. The little girl looked at me,

her mother put her down, and Ursula came to my seat, and said, "I guess we are sisters, or rather half-sisters. Wow, I can hardly believe it—looks like we have the same mother, but different fathers." I got up, put my arms around the surprised Ursula and stumbled, fighting the tears.

"I always wanted to have a sister, someone I knew belonged to me; now I have a family. I can't believe it's true. I have a sister. I have found what I was looking for for so long. I believe that this is a real breath of destiny that I found you."

"I am still shocked. I have to get us some coffee, and we can talk." Ursula introduced me to her two children. "That's Brian; he's four and a heap of trouble. And that's Karin; she's eighteen months and a sweetheart."

Before I knew it, Brian sat on my lap and hugged me, looked at me, and asked, "Did you bring me a toy?" His brown eyes looked at me questioningly, and he was down on the floor trying to look in my purse.

"Brian, stop it! Go and play in your room. She'll bring you a toy the next time she visits, okay?" Brian looked at me shortly, and his small figure disappeared into the next room.

"But I want a robot to play with; bring me a robot," he hollered from the next room.

"I am sorry; he's very demanding right now," Ursula told me, and to the door, "Brian, be quiet for a while, or you won't get a robot."

"Can you hold Karin for a minute, so I can get us some coffee and cake?" Ursula walked out, and I suddenly had a little girl sitting on my lap, looking at me with questioning blue eyes, sticking her wet finger in my mouth and seconds later trying to put it in my eyes. I put

Karin down and let her go, and she crawled right to my purse, sat down, and inspected the contents of it.

"Can she break something in there?" Ursula asked, coming in with a tablet with goodies.

"No, she's fine, just let her play with it. You have beautiful children. Is your husband at work? What did he say about us?"

"Well, we talked about it a little bit after your call, and he wasn't surprised about me having a sister or brother, the same as me—it wouldn't surprise me if we have more sisters or brothers as secretive as our mother always was and still is."

We talked for an hour. I found out that Ursula grew up with her real father, a stepmother and half sister, and also that we grew up not even an hour away from each other. She didn't know about me, and I didn't know about her. Her father was engaged to our mother, but when he came home unexpectedly from the war for a couple of days he found out that our mother was pregnant with someone else's child, he broke the engagement instantly. She also believed that there might have been another child, a son. Ursula told me about her childhood, which was as horrible as mine, only that she could look forward to having her own father coming home from the war one day.

I told her about the circumstances of finding out about her, my upbringing, my surroundings, and how I ended up in Munich. She told me about her marriage, that it wasn't a good one and that she was trying to decide if she should get a divorce or not. She loved her children but had to live with an abusive husband who liked to drink and get physical when drunk. She had wanted to get out of her situation at home and had said yes to the first boy that came along, regretting it ever since.

"I think you better go for today, but if you want, you can come back tomorrow after ten in the morning, so that we can talk more and maybe get out of the house, too. I'd love to hear more from you, and I know you have some more questions, too. My husband doesn't want anything to do with my family; he's under the opinion that my mother was a whore and never wants her in his house. He was not very supportive when I told him I wanted to get to know you and that I always wanted a sister."

"I did too. I always had the feeling that there was someone I missed." I told Ursula about my recurring dream at the main train station and my always wondering about that dream.

We looked at each other, and with tears in our eyes, we stood up and hugged each other.

"Stop it now," Ursula mumbled. "I am glad you found me and tell that nice man at the police station that he's invited for a cup of coffee and cake someday when I come to Munich to visit you."

We said our goodbyes and promised to meet the next day at the KaDeWe (Kaufhaus des Westens), the oldest, most exclusive shopping center close to the Kuhdamm, which used to be, before the division of West and East Berlin, the most prestigious street in Berlin.

Confused, tired, and elevated with happiness I walked back to the apartment. Berlin with all its activity calmed my nerves—the people sitting outside the cafe chatting, the man playing the old organ to solicit money, the buses stopping to pick up tired shoppers, the ever pecking and flying pigeons, the shops with their exclusive layouts, the smell of fresh coffee, the Gedächtniskirche with its blue Chagall windows, and the lipstick-shaped tower beside the ruin of the old church, all gave Berlin the ambience no other city had and brought back sentimental feelings of my time spent there.

My Half Sister

...o; I think he likes you
see each other."
John" as he introduced
... and I was careful not
...ater. He got a big box
...me after we set down
the others go up again
...e of the United States
...romantic movie; we just
...t his hand came over
...nd; it felt good. After
... bar again, but I made
... go home. He brought
...ove. After our movie
... the snack bar until
...uld like to go out with
... go out and eat, have
...nd myself looking for
... this Saturday, and he
...ad borrowed a car and
... restaurant, which also
...onversation was mostly
... and broken English
... time, especially taking
...the park. He was a gen-
...e away from the post
...ight, we exchanged our
...on the weekends, if he
... and I got to know him
...ing of nothing else than
...nd it was three month
...his knees, in front of the

LOVING AGAIN

My time in Munich came suddenly to an end. Over time I had recognized that something was wrong with my health. I was constantly very tired and exhausted, had no appetite, and had lost weight. Helga insisted that I made a doctor appointment, and a very short time thereafter, I found myself in a sanatorium for tuberculosis patients. Driving there with an ambulance car, I didn't get to see much from my new surrounding until much later after I was allowed to get outside the hospital room. The whole site was beautiful, and it seemed to be located right in the middle of a forest. A huge castle-like building with I don't know how many rooms, beautiful grounds with water fountains, parks, and peacocks running around made me ask myself if I was dreaming it all. I was assigned a room with one more patient, a girl from Düsseldorf. She was not very talkative and most of the time we were sedated and ready only to sleep. I remembered only from the first days that someone said, "Don't try to wander off; the whole property is gated with people there to catch you and bring you back. You are a danger to others; that's why we have to keep you away from them."

The shadows on my lungs were treated with rest, good food, shots, and a lot of medication. Outside visitors were only allowed every fourteen days on the weekends. If caught sunning yourself or smoking, the weekend visitation privileges were taken away. This regimen lasted for eighteen months with only Helga coming to visit twice. When I asked why she didn't come more often, she told me that she's afraid she might catch my illness. A doctor reassured her that she couldn't get it anymore, but nevertheless, she stopped coming altogether. Shortly before I was to be released from the sanatorium I got a letter from Helga. The one that I have been through with so much wrote me that she had given my room to another girl and that I could pick up my belongings. I was shocked and couldn't believe it. Was it because the long time I was gone or was she still afraid of the illness? I would find out, I promised myself. We were friends for so long? I was very confused and sad.

My release day came closer, and I asked around if anyone knew about someone renting out rooms in the area. The health insurance had paid me a lump sum for the time spent in the sanatorium, and I had the money for a train ticket to Munich and back, rent for two month, and some furniture if I couldn't find something furnished. Searching through the local newspaper, I had found, shortly before my release, a furnished apartment not far away from the sanatorium. It was a room upstairs in a house, with the owners occupying the ground floor. It was enough for me.

Released at last from the sanatorium in Langendamm, I had my little bag in my hand and was driven to the main train station and on the way to Munich. I had to change trains in Hannover and arrived in Munich around noon. Riding the subway and the streetcar to Theresienhöhe,

I realized how much I had missed Munich and hated to think that I had to move on again. Helga was still at work when I turned the key to the apartment. Nothing had changed, only that my belongings were scattered around the side table and a letter with my name on it on top of it. I sat down, read it, and put it back together again. She wrote how sorry she was that our relationship came to a sudden end, but financially she needed a roommate, and she would always be afraid to get what I had, afraid to hug me and be around me. I could call her anytime and to please slide the key under the door after I locked it. She wished me a lot of luck and hoped that I find a better friend soon.

I locked the door, pushed the key under the door, and drove back to the main train station with two big suitcases, a couple of purses around my neck and my purse over my arm. I wanted to drive to Helga's workplace first, confront her, and tell her what I thought of her, but I changed my mind. What for? She had to fight her own demons, and I have to realize that this part of my life was over and I am alone again.

I had a little time before the train left and stopped at the café for coffee and pastry. When it was time, I got help with my suitcases to put them in the net above the seats and got comfortable. A woman about my age sat opposite me and started to make small talk. I wasn't really in the mood but answered her questions. I found out that she was living in Langendamm and was married with a girl. *It's a small world,* I thought. I told her that I found a room with nice people there, and she knew them. She told me that the homeowners' son used to live in the room that's now mine and that he was in the

Bundeswehr (army) now. She talked and talked; I must have fallen asleep when suddenly I heard her: "We have to get out, we are in Hannover." I mumbled a thank you and grabbed the suitcases. She helped again, and I explained that I was sick a long time and still exhausted, that's why I fell asleep. We went together to the connecting train, and when we arrived in Langendamm, we were like friends, chatting and laughing. I liked her and even got used to her constant talking; it made me forget for a while all my problems ahead. She brought me all the way to the door and told me that she would stop by tomorrow to see if she could help with something. I found out that she lived just two streets away. When I ask if she knew about any jobs being available in the near vicinity; sure enough she did. "They need someone in the snack bar at the army post close by."

I looked disappointed. "I don't speak English."

"Oh, never mind that, you will learn it when you're behind the counter and the soldiers ask you all kind of questions—that's the best way to learn. I'll go with you if you want me to; I speak a little English, okay? I'll get you tomorrow and you see; I bet you get the job." She left and I wanted only to sleep, which I did until the sun woke me the next morning.

I stretched, sat down on the bed's edge, and told myself that all of it is not so bad after all. *I have a room, I have money, and if I am lucky a job. I'll make the best of it.* After I got dressed I went downstairs to see my landlady. Her husband was working in the back where they had a garden with vegetables, flowers, and fruit trees. I gave her the money for the first month rent, and she asked if I needed something and that she wanted to supply the towels and bed stuff also. I thanked her and told her that Bridget would stop by and that she wanted to go with me inquiring for a job on the army post close by. Upstairs again, she called me to let me know that Bridget was there.

We walked to the army post, which was really just around the corner. The chatterbox (that's what I called Bridget secretly) was going thousand miles an hour, and I only had to say "yes" or "no" sometimes. Entering the post, a guard stopped us, and Bridget told him that we wanted to ask about the job. He pointed us to a barrack straight ahead. I saw about seven similar barracks farther away and houses around them, which I thought to be the living quarters for the soldiers. Bridget told me that there are maybe forty American soldiers stationed here who teach the German soldiers some things; she didn't know what. We reached the barrack, entered, and asked for the person who did the job interviews. A sergeant introduced himself (I forgot the name), and we were seated in a room and the door closed. Bridget with her broken English asked if the job was still available and if I could have it. The sergeant asked her something, he looked at me, and asked me something. I only looked at Bridget when she told me to say "tomorrow," so I did, and he told her some more and out we were again.

"What in heaven's name was this all about?" I asked her coming out the post.

"You start tomorrow at 0800 (army time), which means eight a.m. sharp and report to the same sergeant. He will tell you everything you need to know and show you around."

"Are you crazy? I don't understand a word of English.

How do I supposed to get along with them? You are not there—who can I ask if I don't understand?"

"Ah, don't worry, just say always 'okay' or 'no,' which means 'Ja' and 'Nein' or 'I don't understand,' which means you don't understand. I bet you will always have someone who speaks German in the bunch; remember, it's a German/American post."

"I don't know if I can do this. I know they have different kind of money that I have never seen, and I know they eat different things from what I have seen in the movies. I'll be lost with no one to ask for help."

"Don't be scared; everything will work out. Just believe in yourself, and you will see by the end of next week you will feel differently."

"I don't know yet if I should thank you for helping me to get this job. I'll let you know next week, all right?"

We shook hands and went back to my apartment, talked a little, and she invited me to her place. It was a similar house to the one I lived in, two stories with the top one being hers. She showed me around; there was a nice bedroom, a kitchen with a seating area, a bathroom, and a living room. She showed me pictures of her husband and her little girl, who was in school right now. She told me about her husband, that he liked to drink and get physical when drunk. She showed me her latest bruises all over her arms, on her neck, and on her legs where he kicked her. She is listening around what she would have to do to get a divorce without him knowing about it. He would never let her have their daughter, and she would need to move away somewhere so he couldn't find her. She was figuring this out right now and was thinking about her parents, to stay with them since they didn't liked him from the beginning and he didn't know where they live.

Time went by, and she begged me to leave before her daughter and husband came home, otherwise she would be in trouble. I left and she told me that she would come by as soon as she could. At the apartment again, the landlady had left some fruits on the table. I ate some, set my alarm clock, and got ready for bed. It took a while before I could settle down; too many things went through my head. Could I hold the job, could I learn English fast enough, or would the people get impatient with me and fire me? No matter what, I knew I would do my best to keep the job.

At 0800 the next morning I walked into the post again and was directed to the same sergeant again. Filling out paperwork, which was to my luck in German and English, getting an ID card, and then I was directed to follow him to the snack bar. I saw a small room with six tables on one side and a bar on the other. Snacks, cakes, newspapers, candy, chewing gum, sodas, and a coffee station were located behind the bar. Toward the tables, behind a glass bar several big metal bowls that were holding hot stuff, like bacon, hash browns, scrambled eggs, and biscuits. And a scary thing to me—the cash register. Some of the food I hadn't seen before I wasn't concerned with, but the money, which I had no idea how to handle because I never seen it before, scared me. The sergeant pointed at several things, talked, and introduced me to Sam, an American soldier working also in the snack bar. It was very quiet right now, and the sergeant left, leaving me with Sam, who to my big surprise could talk a little German. He had to explain what the sergeant all had told me, he did in his broken German, but at least I know what was going on. He explained that I was responsible to take care of filling up everything, the cash register, and keeping the tables and the dining area in tip-top shape. The cooking and breakfast serving is his thing and also cleaning that area at night. I was very nervous when the first customers came in asking for breakfast and the newspaper. Thank God for pointing, that's what it was at first, people just pointing to things they wanted, and if I just didn't understand, I went to asked Sam, who usually stayed in the back and left the whole front to me. The money part he had explained shortly; I wrote down what all the coins were about and the paper money he showed me from the cash register. I was afraid that I might give too much money back and at night I would be responsible for it. I don't remember much from the first days and was always happy I had survived another day. After a week Bridget came in to see how I was doing. She got some coffee and pastry and watched me for a while. "Don't you have anything better to do than sit there and make me nervous?" I asked her.

"Didn't I tell you, wait a week and you will do fine? And I can tell you are okay, you are doing fine. I came to ask you if you want to go to the movies with me on Sunday night since you don't have to work; my husband went with my daughter to his parents," and I am alone."

"Sounds good, I see you on Sunday at five p.m."

She left again. Sunday came, and we went on the way to the movies. I was surprised when she stirred me to the post again. "What are you doing? There is no movie theater on post!"

"Yes, there is, and I thought it wouldn't hurt both of

us if we see an American movie, this way we learn more English. How hard can it be? Seeing the pictures explains a lot, and seeing American actors/actresses is interesting. I think that's the only way to get to know another culture and people from other countries. That's always fascinating, don't you think? They even take German money to get in; how about that?"

"You have done your homework, didn't you? Okay, let's see how much we can understand from the movie." We paid, looked a little stupid at the concession stand and that machine that spit out some white little things and the big bags and drinks people took into the movie. We had no idea what that white stuff was, went into the dark movie, walking down an aisle, and I found myself suddenly on the floor. I had slipped on the greasy floor, which I later found out was common from the popcorn that had fallen on the floor and not cleaned up properly. I experienced my first American movie with my behind hurting. Barely sitting down, everyone was getting up again and holding their right hand over their heart: "I pledge allegiance to the flag of the United States of America and to its republic for which…" The whole movie theater was talking about something I couldn't understand until into the far future when I would use the same words. The movie was a Western, we both didn't understand much from the words, but the scenes showed what it was all about. A rancher had gotten too big and turned into a bad guy, buying of all the land around, and started to ration water for the rest of the people, who finally stood up to him and killed him. For the first time we saw cowboys and what they do, saw a tremendous landscape with wide open places, and saw how people lived in this strange environment.

Life went on with working and working until one day Bridget asked me to go with her out to have some fun. I agreed, and she guided me again to the post. "Is there nothing around here other than the post we can go to?" I asked her.

"There is, but I want you to get better in your English so that you don't feel discouraged when you don't understand something."

"Nice of you, but I have enough being all day on post and don't feel like going in the evening back there."

"Come on; see what it is all about when the Americans have fun." She guided me to a barrack, then into a long hallway to a room with a lot of tables and chairs, a bar, a music box, and soldiers with beer bottles in their hands. People were dancing to a slow song on the very small dance floor. We tried to find a table as one soldier came and took Bridget's hand and showed her to sit down with another soldier at their table. We sat, ordered sodas, and looked at each other stupidly. The soldiers spoke a little German and our communication slowly made sense. We danced a lot and found out where the soldiers were from. One was from Alabama, the other from Georgia. They wanted to know if we could meet again since they had to leave in a little bit. We agreed and left for the night. Bridget tried to find out which one I liked from the two; they were so different. "I like the one from Alabama. He has pretty eyes, and I love his hands, like doctor hands, so fine and small. I don't know about the dancing; I guess he was a little tipsy already. What do you think about him?"

"He's cute, but not my type, I liked the other one—I am a nut for dark-haired guys and tall ones. He danced all right, but I think he was tipsy also. We'll see the next time around. Do you want to see them again? We can go to Nienburg in a different club, if you want, but I have to wait until my husband has a tour out of town again and is gone for couple of days and my neighbor will watch my little girl."

"I am not in a hurry; that's fine. Thanks for going with me tonight; I see you when I see you. Bye, bye." I went upstairs and went to bed.

Days came and went, and I had almost forgotten about that soldier from Alabama when one day he stood in front of me in the snack bar. "Haben Sie eine Morgenzeitung für mich?" (Do you have the morning paper for me?) He wanted to show me that he had learned a German sentence, but I understood: "Haben Sie Morgen Zeit für mich?" (Do you have time for me tomorrow?). "No" was my only response, and he started pointing to the newspaper. I felt my blood rushing to my head, turned, and ran to the back room. I was so embarrassed. I didn't want to come out until he had left.

A month had gone by when he came into the snack bar again. He smiled at me, got some coffee, and sat down at a table. When he left, he put a note into my hand and the money for the coffee. I opened it, and in German it said: "Tut mir leid das Misverständnis letztes Mal, können wir uns wiedersehen? Vielleicht Sonnabend für einen Film, um 2000 (8:00 p.m.)?" (I am sorry about the misunderstanding the last time. Can I see you again? Maybe on Saturday for a movie at 8:00 p.m.?). I was impressed; he must have had some help with this one.

When I talked to Bridget about it, she was excited

for me and told me: "You better go; I think he likes you. Tell me about it the next time we see each other."

I did go to the movies with "John", as he introduced himself. This time he wasn't tipsy, and I was careful not to slip again walking into the theater. He got a big box of this white stuff and offered some after we set down. Unusual, I thought when he and the others got up again for: "I pledge allegiance to the flag of the United States of America ..." This time it was a romance movie; we just watched and didn't talk at all, but his hand came over to get a hold of mine. I didn't mind; it felt good. After the movie, he wanted to go to the bar again, but I made myself understood that I wanted to go home. He brought me to the door, and we said good-bye. After our movie together, there were a lot of visits to the snack bar until one day again he ask me if I would like to go out with him. He wanted to go to Nienburg, go out and eat, have a drink or two. I agreed and caught myself looking forward to it. I didn't have to work this Saturday, and he picked me up around noon. He had borrowed a car and had made arrangements at a fine restaurant, which also offered dancing later on. Our conversation was mostly with pointing, drawing, showing, and broken English and German. We had a wonderful time, especially taking a walk after the dancing in the nearby park. He was a gentleman and a different person when away from the post. After he brought me home that night, we exchanged our first kisses that night. From then on, the weekends, if he didn't had duty, we spent together, and I got to know him better, falling in love and thinking of nothing else than him. Our relationship got deeper, and it was three month later when John suddenly got on his knees, in front of the people in the snack bar, and asked me to marry him. The soldiers in the room started yelling and screaming, "Yeah! Hurray! Go for it!"

With tears in my eyes, I said: "Yes, I love to marry you."

Shortly after I asked my landlady if John could move in with me, she was happy for me and opened another room so that we had two rooms for us for the same rent. I was happy through and through. John had gotten permission to live off post and had started the paperwork that we could get married. Time went by with physical examinations, talking to the post commander: "Why I wanted to marry an American." Then it was a conversation with the chaplain from the post with the same question and more. A long waiting time started until I found out that I was pregnant. A love child for both of us, John was nervous and excited; he wanted us to be married before the baby was born. I was three months pregnant when we finally, after eighteen months, got permission to get married. After the country clerk office (Standesamt), we went to a small hotel, where we had stayed before and celebrated with Bridget and her husband and the people who owned the hotel. It was November 2, 1970.

In the six months until the birth of our baby, we moved into quarters assigned by the Americans, bought some furniture for it (from the money I still had from the health insurance), and had everything ready for the baby. I stopped working a month before the baby was due, and we were the happiest parents ever when in May, 1971, our baby girl was born. Just in time to get ready, since her dad got transferred to Fort Hood, Texas, with six weeks of vacation before reporting there on September 12, 1971.

t have to worry about
very shy."
I was surprised when
to sit with him in his
through the windows
near. He looked at me
with him listening to
followed by Creedence
the Rain," which was

sat for a while when he
at my wedding ring.
as engaged to be mar
I understood very well
before it sunk in that he
e in Duncanville. I was
get out of the car and
could not believe what
ost; tears were running
away and kept on walk-

had been walking when
husband's brother got
nt of me to make me
down, and my husband
do you think you are
plain. I love you. Will
walking. The car finally
stop.
begged. Like a zom-
rdered. It was a while

IMPRESSIONS

JULY 1971

The time we would be traveling from Germany to the United States of America seemed unreal, a fathomless number of hours. From Hannover to Frankfurt, from Frankfurt to O'Hare, Chicago, from O'Hare to Birmingham, Alabama, and a four-hour drive from Birmingham to Duncanville outside of Tuscaloosa. My marriage to an American soldier would bring me and my baby girl, after the visit in Duncanville, to an army town in Texas, where my husband would have to report to duty on September 12. We would spend the first two weeks at his parents' house and then continue with a fourteen-hour drive to Texas. This journey would bring me pain and doubts, a miscarriage, new impressions, a big family, and a strange welcome from Mother Nature.

From Frankfurt, Germany, to O'Hare, Chicago, I was clutching my ten-week-old baby girl close to me, passing her into the arms of my husband when the pain in my uterus started again. The shot from the German doctor had taken effect, causing me to miscarry in mid-air, a new life that was determined unwelcome, conceived too early after the birth of my baby girl. The trips to the bathroom, without my baby, but with her Pampers clutched to my side, continued until we reached Chicago. The questioning looks of the passengers, the unsuccessful attempts to rest, the big screen showing Albert Hitchcock's movie *Marnie,* and seeing the constant life of the ocean below destroyed all attempts of calming my nerves. Anxiety, fear, and anticipation changed in sequence but seemed to escalate the closer we got to the end of our flight. My frequent hopeful looks at my husband to find a little sympathy or support were left unanswered. He had periodically assured me that, as a German woman, I would be able to handle anything. Germans are strong, loving, stubborn, and born to carry the weight of the world on their shoulders. Coming back from another trip to the bathroom, I stopped and looked at my little family. My husband's sandy hair, the blue eyes that could both make me think loving thoughts and put a touch of doubt in my heart, his hands that could be doctor's hands—small and fine, but strong—the uniform that was required for travel. I thought he was handsome. Every time I looked at him, I felt the same sensation of love that enveloped me since the beginning of our relationship. We wanted a child very much, and there she was, our beautiful little angel with rosy cheeks, a hat covering the hairless little head, her little hands formed into fists, who was sleeping through it all, obviously without a worry in the world. The intervals between bathroom visits finally shortened, and I started to relax a little.

"This is the captain speaking; we will be landing shortly at O'Hare Airport. I hope you had a pleasant flight and thank you for choosing American Airlines," interrupted my dozing and was followed by the usual announcements of the stewardess to fasten your seatbelts and put your seats to the upright position. My German friend's saying suddenly entered my mind—the starts and landings are the most dangerous moments when flying. Assuring that my baby girl was securely in her seat, waking up my sleeping husband and grabbing his hand, I envied the calmness of both when the plane touched the ground and came to a screeching halt. We had made it to the United States of America. Elated, I hugged my husband and was able to put anxiety and fear aside for a while.

"Are you really going to kiss the ground, as you told me you would?" I asked him.

As he was bending down, he said, "Watch me," and kissing the ground, he stopped the flow of passengers behind us. Touched by his gesture I was wondering if I would be feeling the same way one day going back to Germany.

"We need to find our connecting flight. Come on," my husband mumbled, pushing me to go on. It was then that I suddenly realized, *I am in a different country.* Everywhere, English—the directional signs, the writing on the shops, the overall airport sounds, and the chatter of the people around us. Everything looked strange, food I have not seen before, names of drinks I had never heard before, magazines I could not read yet, and I could not understand the sales lady behind the counter asking me what I want. I was forced, as so many times before, to recognize the shortcomings of not being fluent in the language, barely understanding it, looking for translation to my husband whose only remark was: "I told you to go to evening classes to learn more English."

Another flight and we finally landed in Birmingham, Alabama. By now we were so exhausted that we just wanted it to be over, no more airports, no more planes, no more tired faces passing by in a trance, but we had to overcome one more obstacle. My husband's brother was supposed to pick us up at the Delta check-in counter, but no one was waiting for us. An hour later two brothers were falling into each other's arms, and I was introduced. He had a Dr Pepper in his hand, blue eyes like my husband's, wild hair, jeans a size too big, and he looked tired and as if he just had come from working in a field. I felt wandering eyes going over me and my baby girl, making me feel insecure, but I was too tired to think anything of it. I was choked by the hot air, coming out of the airport, making breathing difficult. I had never experienced a heat such as that and was worried, hoping that my baby girl would be able to tolerate such temperatures.

"I cannot believe this heat," I mumbled, walking to his brother's car. The maroon, old Buick was loaded with our luggage, my husband sat in the front, and I stretched out on the unbelievably comfortable backseat with my baby. It was diaper and feeding time again and once done, she gave me a look of satisfaction, arms stretching and yawning wholeheartedly. Shortly after she went to sleep again and I had the chance to look out of the window. Buildings flew by, red lights, the feel of busy people on sidewalks and in cars made me think that I could be in Berlin driving down the street on Kuhdamm or Hohenzollerndamm. Only the voices from the front seat reminded me that we were in a different country. Comfortable seating and the comfortable climate because of the air conditioning (a very important commodity to have, I found out) made the voices from the front seat turn into mumbling and then a whispering, and before I knew it I was asleep.

A car's angry horn woke me, and my husband told me that we were getting close to his home. *Good,* I thought. Remembering what he had told me about his parents and his home, I felt admiration, disbelief, love, and respect for his parents. They had raised twelve children, and I could not wait to meet them. He had told me that they lived on a big farm in a nice brick house on a lot of land, that he had eight brothers and three sisters, that one of the twelve children had polio and always stayed at home, and that I would love the countryside and his parents. I was told that we were in Tuscaloosa and had to drive about thirty more minutes. The road cut through beautiful fields of green and white dots, which were hugged by tremendous pine forests that reached periodically up to the edge of the street. It was afternoon, hot, and it seemed like nature held its breath, no birds were singing, no breeze, just the glare from the heat on the road. Several deer stood very still on the edge of the forest looking at us before we came to a turn in the road. A huge, beautiful brick house on the slope of a hill came into view, a dirt road beside it going up the hill through fields of cotton, then a big field with different vegetables most of which I did not know, then an old shack of a house on top of the hill. Thick forest behind and on both sides formed the background, giving the feeling of security and comfort. To the south of the house the beautiful landscape was made up of fields and forests covered by the flaming evening sky, ready to be a choice for any artist longing to find a perfect landscape. Two lonely houses parked in the glory of God's beauty.

I was still breathless from all this beauty when the Buick came to a stop and was suddenly surrounded by a lot of people laughing, pushing, and crying. Everyone ganged up on my husband, hugging him, kissing him, and passing him from one to another. I knew that it had to be my mother-in-law that hugged my husband now with tears running down her cheek. An elderly man, I assumed to be my father-in-law, kept his distance, leaning on an old Ford and looking upon all the excitement with a seemingly bored interest. Not understanding half of the conversations, I stayed in the car, waiting until my husband would get me. Periodically he pointed at me telling his family who-knows-what about me, and then he came and helped me out of the car.

I was checked out by at least eighteen pair of eyes and was pushed aside as they took a look at my baby girl.

"Look at her. She's gorgeous. She's beautiful. She's so tiny. I think she smiled at me. I want to hold her. Let me see her and look at these cute clothes." I watched closely and was ready to intervene at the smallest hint of danger to my little angel. My mother-in-law glanced at me, and I pointed to the house, wanting to get inside in the hope of escaping the smoldering heat. My husband glanced at me and understood; he started moving slowly toward the house with everyone following him. A door opened up into a kitchen with the biggest dining table I had ever seen. A huge stove, ready to handle this big family, cabinets and chairs, chairs, chairs. Four bedrooms, I had been told, one of which was ready for us to get some rest, but first I had to see the rest of the house. I pinched my husband letting him know that I needed to use the bathroom. He pointed at one of his sisters to show me where to go—outside again, she pointed at a small wooden house, pressed newspaper into my hand, and opened the door to the "bathroom." As I entered, the smell, the heat, and the flies made my stomach turn, and I instantly vomited when I was outside again. I decided to use the company of the huge pine trees and nature the next time the need arose.

The family had hung around for a couple of hours, disappearing slowly, when my husband finally steered us toward our bedroom. A big bowl of water on the dresser, a chair, clothes hangers on a nail behind the door, and a bed made up our room. Exhausted, I asked, "Where can I take a shower?" I received only a questioning look from my husband. I was so tired that I attended quickly to my daughter's needs, put her in the middle of the bed, and lay down beside her. Instantly, I was asleep. The next morning, the smell of something baking and people talking in the kitchen woke me up. I felt sand under my body, and taking the sheet off the bed, I went outside to shake it out. My mother-in-law came from the "bathroom" smiling.

"These dumb dogs are always on the beds; we can't stop them."

Our breakfast with my in-laws and two brothers-in-law consisted of coffee, biscuits, and beans. Albert, the only child that had contracted polio, limped and slobbered around my daughter's baby buggy, and the unimaginable heat early in the morning put me in a somber mood. My husband had left to see friends and family he has not seen in years, leaving a message that he would be back soon.

After taking care of my daughter's needs, I used the time to study the gentle face of my mother-in-law. Conversation was very limited and consisted of showing, pointing, and "yes" or "no." She attended to her needlework in front of the fireplace, got up frequently to spit a brown mass into it, and sat down again. I looked at her very worried and could not wait until my husband came home to ask him about this unusual behavior. Later we moved outside to the front porch where a little breeze brought relief from the heat. My mother-in-law was sitting opposite from me, lifting her head every now and then looking at me and the baby and again with questioning eyes turning back to her needlework. I wished she would ask and I could answer her questions. Her face was marked with laugh lines but also a harshness that reminded me of hard times. Her eyes seemed to look right into your heart, searching for the core of the human being. Her hands, big and covered with scabs, made me wonder if she was in pain doing that needlework. A big apron covered her big body, and her hair, the color of dirty snow, was tied in the back into a knot. She must have felt my spying eyes and asked:

"Do you love my boy?"

"I surely do, Mom" was my response, happy that I understood and could answer. Her husband had left for the town, leaving us with Albert and my daughter. Getting to know my father-in-law better had to wait until his return. Mute Albert limped around the front yard, picking up things, grinning at us, or groaning words only his mother could understand. A wave of admiration hit me again for his parents who had done the best they could by working the land for the landlord living down the hill in the beautiful house. It baffled my mind and made me sad that my husband thought that he had to paint a picture of his parents and his family different from reality. Shouldn't he be proud and full of admiration for his parents who had worked so hard to raise all their children? His tale, when in Germany, that his family had a lot of land and a brick house meant, by German standards, that his family was financially secure. Shortly thereafter I learned a new word—sharecroppers—meaning that the land and the house did not belong to them, that they worked the land for the landowners. My parents-in-law supported their family by keeping what they needed of food from working the land and lived rent free in the house. Meat was made available from hunting, and money needed came from the sell of the homemade "moonshine," produced deep in the woods of Duncanville. Moonshine was one of the many new words I learned; to my own detriment, I had to taste it, instantly wishing I had not! Two sips of it gave me the feeling of experiencing hell on earth; a burning flame traveling through the whole body made me wonder why anyone would like to drink this devil's brew voluntarily.

One evening when we sat all together, I remembered the unusual behavior from my mother-in-law spitting into the fireplace. I winked my husband to come outside, eager to find out about it.

"I am very worried, John. I saw your mom spitting a brown mass several times a day into the fireplace, and she did it also when she was outside. She must be very sick; does she have to take medication; what is wrong with her?" He looked at me and started laughing, harder and harder.

"What is wrong with you? What are you laughing about?" I wanted to know.

Gasping, he said, "She is not sick; she is chewing tobacco. Have you never heard of people chewing tobacco?"

"No, well, at least she is not sick." I felt better already, and we walked back to the house where he had to tell about my questions, making everyone break out in laughter.

It was in Duncanville, Alabama, that I was introduced to the grandeur of nature, the wideness of the land, the hours of nothing but streets, forest, sunshine, dust, and heat. These reddish dust roads, leading through hours of forest, became an exhilarating experience, driving up and down like on a roller coaster, making it impossible to see what lay ahead before a steep way led us down again. These rides into the forests in the old Buick ended usually at a waterhole for a relaxing and refreshing dive into the cool waters. Surrounded by the smell of pines, the singing of birds, and the rays of the sun peeking through the trees often set the stage for relaxing and loving thoughts and actions amid this beauty.

Reality soon brought us back to the house of his parents for an evening meal of biscuits and beans and to our lovely baby daughter who had been carried around my mother-in-law's neck in a sort of apron with a big pocket. Six of her children were at the house when we got back, giving me the chance to look at them closely. All had the family resemblance, some had different hair colors and textures, some had dark eyes, but most of them had the blue eyes like my husband. I had heard that one married a drunk, one a wife abuser, one worked in the woods, and some drove huge trucks for lumber companies. Not to forget the ones who produced that devil's drink moonshine. After dinner most of her children disappeared one after another to be with friends or to go hunting.

For the first time my father-in-law sat at the table with us. His children and his wife seemed to be used to his silence. He dipped his biscuits into a bowl of gravy, spooned up butterbeans, and followed with a drink from this Budweiser bottle. In a monotonous way his strong hands repeated these motions until his meal was gone. My curious eyes noticed bushy eyebrows, sunken cheeks, piercing eyes, and small, hard lips. No laugh lines were around the eyes, only lines that gave evidence of a hard life, lines that could tell stories of pain, hunger, giving up, but recuperating every day to face the next. I did not once see him smile during the two weeks we were in his house. He was there for the meals and attended to his chores after it. In the evening he sat in his old Ford, drinking his Budweiser, or drove off to visit friends or family that lived either in Duncanville or in the woods around it. Some of the family members came to visit in the evening, sitting on the porch, talking, drinking, or just looking around. These evenings were ceremonial and repetitious, but relaxing and kind of calmed down the nerves before bedtime.

It was in the middle of the night when nature called. I took some newspaper, put on my shoes, and tried to find a spot between the pines. The stars seemed so close that I felt I could grab one if I wanted to. The moon put a strange light on everything, making the edge of the forest appear closer and alive. Shadows came and went, but wait. What was that? Something moved quietly toward me; I heard twigs breaking under its paws. It looked like a cat, but I knew cats were not that big. I could not move; I froze, making no noise at all. The big cat was about fifteen feet away from me when it suddenly stopped, looked around, and as if spooked by something, turned around and ran back into the forest. It took me about thirty minutes to collect myself and go back to bed again. When I told my husband about my meeting during the night, he laughed and said, "These mountain lions come around every now and then, look around, sometimes they get a chicken, but otherwise you don't have to worry about them. They are scared of you and very shy."

One evening, after our dinner, I was surprised when my father-in-law waved me over to sit with him in his truck. A little breeze coming through the windows brought relief from the evening heat. He looked at me and said, "You like this music?" I sat with him listening to Johnny Cash's "I Walk the Line" followed by Creedence Clearwater Revival's "Who'll Stop the Rain," which was one of my husband's favorite bands.

"I like it," I answered him. We sat for a while when he suddenly took my hand and looked at my wedding ring.

"Do you know that my son was engaged to be married before he left for Germany?" I understood very well what he said, but it took a while before it sunk in that he meant to another woman right here in Duncanville. I was quiet, but did not answer him. I got out of the car and started walking down the hill. I could not believe what he had said. I felt betrayed and lost; tears were running down my face. I came to the highway and kept on walking toward the city.

I did not know how long I had been walking when the squeaking Buick from my husband's brother got beside me and tried to get in front of me to make me stop walking. The window went down, and my husband said, "Stop walking, stop. Where do you think you are going? I need to talk to you and explain. I love you. Will you please stop?" I could not stop walking. The car finally pulled in front of me, and I had to stop.

"Come on, get in," my husband begged. Like a zombie still in trance, I did as I was ordered. It was a while before my husband started talking.

"Yes, I was engaged to be married before leaving for Germany, and yes, I wrote her from Germany frequently. When I got to know you, I had only fun in my mind—distraction, one-night stands, and getting drunk. I never thought that I would fall in love with you. The more I got to know you, the more things changed. I caught myself not writing her anymore. I did not know what would happen. I had to find out about my own feelings first, if this was really love, if I felt different before, or was it different now. Strangely enough, during the same time I did not get any letters from her either. Then one evening, you had come to the snack bar with your friends, a guy had put his arm around your shoulder, you were laughing, and it hit me—I was jealous, very jealous. That is when it dawned on me—I loved you, I wanted to be with you, all the doubts were gone. I knew you were the one I wanted to marry and be with the rest of my life. Sounds corny, I know, and now I started fighting with myself. Should I send her a letter, letting her know that I was not going to marry her? I could not, call me a chicken, I put it off and put it off and told myself, 'She is not writing either; maybe she got to know someone else too.' I would tell her when I get back to the U.S., confront her with the reality, which was my plan. That is what I did the Sunday I left you at the house, and you would not believe it—she got married also and had not expected to see me at all. My family did not know about it, and that is why they looked at you with questioning eyes. I am sorry about it and the heartache I caused you. Please forgive me, please."

I could not say anything for a while. Then I answered, "Now a lot of things make sense. The periodic absent-mindedness, the times when you did not have time for me, the times you locked yourself in the bedroom, or the times you got drunk mumbling something about a Tracy and that you were sorry. I am sad that you did not tell me a long time ago. You could have saved yourself some troubling times."

"You mean to say that you would not have left me?"

"I was in love with you the first time you stuttered half in English and half in German trying to invite me to go to the movies with you."

"What a dope I was; I am so sorry. I love you, and I do not ever want to cause you any grief again."

The waterhole was our next stop where we spent loving hours, refreshing, loving, and refreshing again. The drive back to his parents' house was relaxing. The feeling of a problem solved, love reinvented, and the future was looking good.

It was three days before our departure for Texas. All through the day, a blistering heat and quietness hung in the air. No breeze, no birds singing, no sounds at all. My in-laws were sitting outside, four of their grandchildren, between ages two and six, who my mother-in-law watched during the week, were playing around a huge old tree in front of the house. It was about three in the afternoon when my father-in-law walked to his truck and turned on the radio. The announcer talked about bad weather predicted to come this way. I did not know which cities were close to Duncanville, I had only heard about Tuscaloosa. I did not pay any attention and kept on playing with my baby girl. My husband had left with a brother of his to find us a decent car that would bring us to Texas.

"A tornado has been confirmed outside Gillespie County and is traveling south," was the next announcement.

"Can you tell me what a tornado is, and where is Gillespie County?" I asked my mother-in-law.

She looked at me in disbelief. "You do not know what a tornado is? They do not have tornadoes in Germany? Well, you better brace yourself and pray that one does not come our way. You would not like what you see."

"Tell me about it; what is it or what does it do? Is it like a thunderstorm, and did you all have some here before?"

"Let me try to explain it. It is a big dirt cloud that spins around and around and picks up everything in its path. It can be a mile in diameter and can take whole brick houses off the ground and leave the ground clean as if there never was a house. It breaks trees like matches, tosses cars into the air, and dumps them down again, can ruin the harvest of a whole year, cuts off electricity, leaving the area it hit looking like a war zone."

"Can people get killed from it, and what do you do when you see one coming or can you even see it?"

"Girl, we are on top of a hill, we can see it coming, unless it comes from behind us and the only thing to do when you see one coming is to get everyone together and huddle around the fireplace of the house or find shelter in a storm cellar and pray."

"Do you have a storm cellar, and where is it?"

"No, we do not have one, but relax; we all know what needs to be done. We have been through several of them and know what to expect."

Hearing the radio talking about this tornado, I got nervous.

"Where is it now? Is it still coming our way? Are we south of it?"

"If it is coming our direction, we will definitely see it soon enough because south is straight ahead, across the highway."

"What about John and Richard? Do they always have the radio on? Do they know that a tornado might come this way?"

"Do not worry; they are used to tornadoes and know to stay away if it comes this way. They will find someone they can stay with in case of danger."

"Should we leave, just in case?"

"Take it easy, so far we have not heard anything we have not heard before. We are not in danger. Not yet anyway."

My mother-in-law kept on knitting and seemed not the least concerned about anything. Albert limped to his daddy, told him something in his own language, and went out to the "bathroom." The children wanted something to drink, so I went inside, checked in on my baby who was sleeping peacefully, and grabbed some lemonade and glasses for them. The kitchen was stuffy, and the old refrigerator moaned and groaned, working overtime. One more check on my baby, I moved the fan away from her little face and out I went again. Stepping out of the door, I held my breath, what was this? It got almost dark outside at four in the evening? I looked at my in-laws and saw concern on their faces for the first time.

"What is going on? Why is it suddenly getting darker?" Giving the drinks to the children, I turned back to my in-laws and stopped in my step. "Look over there. Look!"

My in-laws turned around and saw behind them, about two miles away, a huge dust cloud turning and turning all the way up into the clouds. We could see a small funnel touching the ground, but getting wider and wider going up into the sky. Dancing back and forth, it moved slowly to the left then to the right again. There was an angry roar coming from the distance, and we saw pieces of wood flying through the air. Darkness had almost set in completely, and I froze again as I always did when something scared me.

I felt a hand grabbing me, pulling me. "Oh my God, which direction is it going to go? Let's get the children, tie up what we can, get the dogs, and let's move everyone inside. Pa, bring the truck behind the house and get the cage for the chicken."

Startled, I grabbed two of the children and pulled them inside the house. "Stay here," I hollered, running back into our bedroom. I got my baby girl and put blankets around her, grabbed her bottle from the refrigerator, took some bottles of water, went back into the living room, told the oldest girl to hold my baby, and ran out again, seeing what I could do. My in-laws were running back and forth, the truck was parked behind the house, a cage full of chickens was put behind the truck, and my mother-in-law grabbed the rest of the children, stopped in the kitchen and collected blankets and bottles on the way. Passing each other, she screamed, "Oh my, oh my, we forgot the dogs. Please get them, please."

Outside it got a lot darker and louder. I almost did not hear the dogs; they were hiding around the corner close to the truck. I tried to lift both and was glad they were small. Then one tried to bite me, but I caught him, too, and I ran inside. Inside, everyone was sitting on the floor around the fireplace. The chairs and small tables were moved outside, nothing but people huddling together, children close to the fireplace and grown ups around them for protection. The noise got overbearingly loud, sounding like a freight train coming toward the house.

My mother-in-law had to scream for us to hear, "Put blankets over you and hold hands; do not let go, and do not try to go outside, and let us pray."

A loud cracking of wood started, noises like metal hitting metal, and suddenly one board from the outside wall was pulled away, then another and another and another. I had never heard such noises of hauling, cracking, screaming, banging, pouring, pulling, and scratching; it was horrifying, and we felt dust and wind pulling on our blankets. Other boards were ripped out of the wall; we expected to be hit by them at anytime. Then suddenly, we all felt a strong suction coming from the fireplace, it felt like someone wanted to suck us through it, out of the house. We were holding on to each other, trying hard not to let go. I felt my hand slipping, pulling away from the four year-old-girl I was holding at my left, heard a faint sound of crying, was it my baby or the child? I grabbed the little arm beside me even harder.

This horror seemed to last for hours. The roaring and howling went on and on and then it finally slowed down, turned away as if a freight train were leaving the station. No one moved; everyone was still in shock and could not believe that it was over. Now we could hear the children crying, coughing, whining, and slowly everyone peeled the blankets away from them. One dirty face after another appeared; we looked at each other and started hugging each other. We were all alive and not hurt, aside from some minor scratches and bruises—it was a miracle.

Everywhere there was dust and dirt, leaves, pine needles, pieces of wood and pieces of metal, some bricks from the fireplace—the whole place was in shambles. We looked around in disbelief, there were no walls anymore around us on three sides; we had been huddling together around the only thing that was left in the living room. Stove and refrigerator were pushed into where a bedroom used to be, the huge kitchen table was nowhere in sight, beds were broken in pieces, and only the wall on the back side of the house was left standing. Dirt, dishes, clothes, broken mirrors, pictures—everything was scattered around, leaving almost nothing intact and very little still usable.

"And it did not even hit us straight on, we only got the outside edge of it," my mother-in-law mumbled, holding her two shivering little dogs.

"Children, come to me, I want to check you over to see if anyone is hurt." And one after the other they came, she looked them over, touched them here and there, and was satisfied with the results.

Her husband came from behind the house. "I have half a tree on my truck, but otherwise I think it will drive. Let's see what we still can save from all this mess and get the children home."

"We will wait right here. People heard and saw what happened, and they will come for their children and help us. I will help you with that tree, and then we'll put whatever we can save into the back of the truck. Are the tires still all right?"

"They are fine, woman, and look what is coming up the road."

Two pickups tried to make their way up the hill, stopping frequently, the drivers getting wood, tree branches, and other debris out of the way, getting back into their car again only to stop again. The owner of the brick house down the hill and one of my brothers-in-law got out of their cars.

"Is everyone all right? No one hurt? Wow, what a mess this twister left behind," I heard the landlord saying.

"Did you have any damage down there?" my father-in-law was asking him.

"Not at all. It went right by my house and hit you barely with its outside edges. You all were very lucky, and let's see what we have to do right now." My in-laws walked around the back, found their "bathroom" thrown into the abyss, their chickens still in the cage only twenty feet from where they left them, the truck with one flat tire, and no place to sleep tonight. I still sat with my baby on the living room floor, still could not believe what had happened, thinking that we could be dead. My husband stood suddenly in front of me, holding his hand out, helping me to get up and took me in his arms.

"Thank God you are not hurt. How is our little angel?"

"Just dirty, dusty, hungry, and cranky; she needs food and a diaper change."

"I brought diapers, milk, and a change of clothes for her, but we have to get some for you later. Luckily, I still had most of our stuff in the back of the Buick. We will sleep in a hotel downtown where you can wash up and rest, and we'll leave tomorrow for Texas. Look at the car I got for us; it is a beauty, nice, and comfortable, but it needs a lot of gasoline." He turned to his parents.

"I am glad everyone is well. I saw the news on television in the drugstore and called the others; they will be here shortly to take you home with them. Tomorrow they will come back and start rebuilding everything. I have been told by Mr. Walters, your landlord, that you will get new appliances and new furniture."

The whole mess suddenly caught up with my mother-in-law, and she sat down on the old Ford steps and started crying, "Oh my Lord, oh my God, you got us through this. I thank you, thank you, thank you, and thank you for having such a caring landlord." The tears kept coming relieving her long-felt pressure and tension.

Her husband stepped over to his truck petting her on the back and head.

"It's all right, Mom. It's all right. Just go ahead, let it all come out."

Darkness settled in and more cars kept coming. Everyone was hugging everyone, happy to see that no one was hurt. Slowly, a whole line of cars made their way down the road, dispersing at the bottom of it. We left, knowing we would meet tomorrow morning again. Tired, but happy to see a bed and a shower, I hurried for the long missed pleasure of it. John changed the baby's diaper and fed her, and she was already fast asleep when I came out. What a luxury, a clean bed without sand and a shower; I was happy.

The day of our departure had come. Driving up that hill to the place where there used to be a house brought back the horror for a short while, but we pushed it aside. Once again we were reassured that we could not be of any help with the rebuilding, that everything was in good hands, and that we would only be in the way. My parents-in-law understood that we would need time in Texas to get settled before John had to report to duty. We said our goodbyes, my mother-in-law started crying again, and my father-in-law gave me a big hug. "You are all right. Take care of yourself, and bring the baby by again!"

Tears ran down my face, I hugged him one more time, turned, and sat in the car waiting for John. Albert came limping, waving with his short arm at me, and groaning something.

"We will see each other again," I promised. Eight hands kept waving when we drove down the hill. One more stop at a gas station, and we were on our way to our next stop—Killeen, Texas.

Driving down the road through this new country, I wondered what impressions the future would bring. The past few weeks had brought a miscarriage, a difficult flight, trust in a partner repaired, a mountain lion, moonshine, a tobacco-chewing mother-in-law, marvelous landscapes, and a survival after a tornado. Lying down in the backseat of his comfortable car, my baby in my arms, I dozed off…

DEATH, KIDNAPPING, CITIZENSHIP

Sonja woke me up; she was hungry and needed attention. The trip seemed never-ending, but John wanted me to see a lot of this great, huge country. I constantly went "ah" and "oh," "Look at this," and "Did you see that?" One of the many strange things, which stayed in my mind, was when we drove through Mississippi and Louisiana. There we often saw little wooden houses, which gave the impression that they would fall apart with the next big storm. But big, beautiful Cadillacs were parked in front. To my way of thinking, you had either an old wooden house and an old banged-up car or a beautiful house with a fancy Mercedes in front of it, but not a wooden shack with a beautiful car out front.

Finally, after an overnight stay in a motel, the trip came to an end when we reached Killeen and Fort Hood. John reported in, and we found a little apartment in Copperas Cove, where we would have to stay until we were assigned quarters by the army. Tired, we just did the most urgent things and went to sleep. The next day meant going shopping, the first time in America for me. Our little princess was cranky, it was very hot, and a lot of people in the store had had the same idea, and seemed to need exactly the same items we needed. The rows of groceries looked strange to me, but John explained what to buy and what not to. My experience in the snack bar helped tremendously; at least I knew about bacon, eggs, biscuits, hamburger meat, and cold drinks. I looked for foods similar to those in Germany, because John loved my German cooking, but without success.

For the first time, I got to know that with air conditioning, a thing unknown in Germany, the heat could become bearable. Going in and out of the heat was always a shock treatment. I had trouble breathing, and it felt as if I had just run into a wall. To my amazement Sonja adjusted pretty fast to this previously-unknown heat. She developed normally, and John was a good father. He even changed diapers and fed her, which was, by German standards, a woman thing. He also did the laundry, or helped in the kitchen.

Soon we got our first home in America: three bedrooms, two baths, a big kitchen, and a back yard, which was huge compared to what I was used to. We had to clean it first, but I quickly turned the house into a home any person would like to come back to. John got his assignment, teaching other soldiers to work with cannons.

We had the seventies, a time of anti-authoritarian protest. John told me often that he was getting tired of telling the soldiers what to do. They said either "No" or "Why?" or "I don't feel like it" so many times that he ended up loading and cleaning the cannon himself. He liked coming home; the dinner was on the table, the house was clean, and after dinner, he could enjoy his six-pack of beer and work on our car. Our marriage seemed, in my opinion, to be a good marriage. I learned what a movie drive-in theater was, how to get money out of a machine without going into a bank, picking up food through a drive-in, got a plastic card to go shopping after being told I do not need real money anymore. When shopping, I came back with vegetables for John to explain what they were used for and to explain how to prepare them. He never got tied of all my questions.

Soon I wanted to help out financially with the bills, so I started working toward my commercial driver's license to become a school bus driver. I was told I could take my baby with me on the runs to pick up and deliver children. I was out of the house only two times a day, leaving enough time to take care of the house and John. It worked out very well. I did not earn very much money, but it helped, and my vocabulary improved also. Many times I came home and asked John to tell me what this word means, and often he told me not to remember this one and not to repeat another—words I had picked up from high school kids on the bus. After my disciplined upbringing in Germany, the lack of discipline of the American children was quite astonishing. Many times I had to stop the bus on the side of the road to make the students stop fighting and screaming. Once I even turned around and went back to the school to talk to the principal, because I was not accustomed to being called names.

One day, on a weekend, Sonja got very sick with a high fever, difficulty breathing, crying, and coughing. I was scared and called to find out if John wanted me to take her to the hospital and if he could meet me there. He had the car, and I would have had to take a taxi. He had told me he was on CQ, meaning he had to stay on post over the weekend. When I finally got someone on the telephone, I was told that John was off duty and he was not there. My mind went blank, and I couldn't understand what I was just told. Where was he? I searched my mind. We did not have any friends he could have stayed with. Was he hurt in some hospital and I did not hear about it yet? Had he been acting differently or did we have any problems I was not aware of?

First was Sonja, I called a taxi and took her to the hospital where they put her in cool water to bring the fever down, gave her a shot so that she could breath better, watched her for a while, and then sent us home again with medication for her. A bad cold had been the trigger for an asthma attack, giving her troubles breathing. I was told that it could happen again, to watch out for signs of difficulties in breathing, then to bring her right away in again. When coming home, I put her to bed, and she fell asleep. I sat and tried to figure out "why" this happened—what had I done wrong? Where was John? I could not find any answers, so I had to wait until he came home and to give me the answers. Sunday evening came; I had put the hospital papers on the table when John walked in. He looked at the papers, asking if Sonja was okay, and sat down. I did not say anything, waiting for him to tell me where he was. He finally broke down and admitted that he was with another woman. I was puzzled. Why? He had a pretty, slender wife, with long blond hair, and a beautiful child. I just could not understand why. We talked and talked, but he kept telling me he loved only me and that he did not know why he did it.

I made him stay on post and live there until I made up my mind if I wanted him back, but I guess that was a mistake on my part. He went back to the other woman, twice my size and the mother of four children. He kept showing up wanting to see Sonja, telling me how much he missed me, and asking if he could take Sonja home to Alabama for a short weekend visit. I did not expect anything bad and let him take Sonja. That turned out to be another mistake. I had found a little apartment and was busy moving when Sunday night came and he was not back from Alabama. I got really worried, thinking they might have had a car accident. I knew he had to be back on post by Monday morning, so I called and asked if my husband had come in yet and said that I needed to talk to him. I was told that he was AWOL (absent without leave) and that disciplinary action was awaiting him on his return. On Tuesday he called and told me that he loved Sonja too much to give her up and that if we separated he would keep her for good, and that he had left her in Alabama. I begged, pleaded, cried, and swore, but nothing helped. After several days, I finally decided, on the advice of my colleagues, to talk to a lawyer. I did and was told that the only way I would get my daughter back was to pretend to make up and move back with my husband again, and then go with him to Alabama and pick her up. The law in Texas could not help me because she was in another state.

Weeks had gone by when, against my better judgment, I agreed, and John called and asked if we could get together and talk. He swore again that he loved only me and that he wanted his family back. We went out together just as we had done in Germany; he was very sweet and tried hard to convince me to come back to him. After he did this several times, I softened and let him move into my little apartment. He was really trying and even considered talking to a marriage counselor. He claimed he could not understand why he did the things he did. He sounded sincere and I started believing him again.

Two months later we went to Alabama together and brought Sonja back. Everything seemed to be perfect again. But I could not forget, and my trust was ruined. I was wondering and worrying when he was gone or had to work on the weekend. I told him about this and we came to the understanding that it was his fault and that he had to earn my trust again. He wanted to prove that he did not need other women by moving into the barracks where he could go out with "his women," meaning Sonja and me. It did not take me very long to find out that all his words were lies when I saw him with the same woman again one day. He swore again and again that I was the only one he loved and always would love. But then he moved in with her again! I did not know what to think anymore. He pleaded, "Please, our third anniversary is coming; let's spend it together one more time, eating, dancing, and being together one last time," and he would never bother me or Sonja again. I could not bring myself to grant him, as it turned out a month later, his last wish.

DEATH

On November 30, 1973, when I got back from my morning run driving the children to school, two men in army uniforms were waiting for Sonja and me. They told me John had been involved in an accident in the field and I needed to come right away with them to Darnell Hospital. In the hospital, I found an unconscious John, each leg being held together in a wooden, half-round shell because his legs were only raw flesh. I talked to him, stroking his forehead and wishing that I had not denied his wish several weeks before. Crying and stroking his head again, he moved his head toward me, making me think that there may be a chance for him to survive. Asking the doctor about it, he told me that it was only a reflex and that he is bleeding too much internally. They did not expect him to live. When coming out of the room to use the bathroom, I could not believe my eyes. The woman who had brought so much pain into my life was coming toward me, begging me to let her see him. I was too perplexed and I let her go in, thinking she must have loved him too. I remembered how John hated hospitals and how he had wished that he never would have to stay longer than a day in one.

After hours of waiting for a miracle, the doctors sent me home. I could not do anything in the hospital, and I had to take care of Sonja. I did not want to leave. I was barely home when the hospital called and told me that John had just passed away. A part of my life had left me. All the bad thoughts were gone, and I only remembered how sweet and loving he could be. I found out later that the anti-authoritarian times and a defective shell were responsible for his death. He had given an order again and was given a stupid answer, so he had loaded the cannon himself. The one responsible for loading it received only slight injuries when the shell exploded in the barrel instead of coming out of the front. John was closest to the cannon when it exploded.

I could not indulge very long in memories. Suddenly

my apartment was full of strangers from Fort Hood: a priest, the detachment commander, a major, and people who wanted to take care of Sonja and me. Sonja just got scared with all the strangers around, and I wanted to be alone with my sorrow so I told all of them to please leave. The army made all the funeral arrangements, and John's parents begged me to have him buried with the other family members in Duncanville, so he was transported to Alabama. I was glad I did not have to make all the arrangements and that a major from the army was sent to stay by my side and take care of everything. The trip to Alabama and back, the funeral, and everything around kept me in a trance for a long time. That John was gone, it was just unbelievable, and I still expected the phone to ring or him to come through the front door any moment.

Financially I would not have to worry, I was told. We would get Social Security, veterans' pension, and maybe life insurance from John.

I had to decide whether I wanted to stay in America or go back to Germany. The army would pay to get everything shipped to Germany if I decided to go back. Long hours of grieving, thinking, and wondering followed. What was the right thing to do? There was nobody in Germany I would like to go back to, but maybe I could have a better life there. One day I wanted to go back, the next day I did not. Finally orders were ready, but before we were due to leave, I changed my mind and decided to try to make a living in America.

CITIZENSHIP

After months in shock, I sat down and tried to figure out which direction I wanted our lives to go. I wanted, first of all, a home I could call my own for the two of us. I found a $17,000 house in Killeen that I liked and bought with the help of the VA (Veterans Administration) loan, and slowly turned the house into a home. Still driving the school bus, I decided the next step would be to find out what I could do about getting a better job. Since my daughter was an American citizen and I had the German citizenship, I wanted to find out what was needed to become an American citizen. Soon I started the paperwork to become a citizen. A lot of learning and a lot of tests for citizenship followed. Neighbors were questioned if, in their opinion, I would make a good citizen, and police records were checked. After I learned everything about the American constitution and how the government works, in April, 1975, I was sworn in as a naturalized American. Now Sonja and I were both American citizens.

New things to learn lay ahead for my daughter and me. I had to learn that there are differences in the way a married woman with a husband and a single mother are treated. The stigma attached to being a single mother seemed to give other people the right to abuse, condemn, and shun them. Suddenly I was not a welcome guest in their homes anymore, and friends with boyfriends started to avoid me altogether. When I chose to stay alone, it was assumed there was something wrong with me or I just could not get a man.

KIDNAPPED AGAIN

I still drove the school bus and started classes in the evening for my GED. One day I received a phone call from John's niece, Emily. She was twenty years old and told me that she could not find a job in Alabama. She asked if she could come and stay with me until she found a job and an apartment in Killeen. I told her that it would be all right, and she came and moved in with us. Sonja was almost four, and Emily took care of her while I drove the bus and went to evening classes. She had been with us now for five months and was still looking for a job.

One evening after I had taken the children home after school, I came home and found Emily tied to the table lamp, crying, and the back door broken in. She told me someone had broken in, taken Sonja, and told her not to call the police or he would kill her. He would call and let me know what he wanted. She cried and blamed herself for not being careful enough. I started feeling sorry for her, but I called the police even though she objected strongly. I did not know what else to do. Several detectives came and hooked up listening devices to the telephones, and a long waiting time started. About 7:00 p.m., Emily came back from the bathroom and said that she had found a note. It said: "Bring $5,000 to the phone booth on Rancier beside the 7 Eleven and put it on the floor. If you don't, I'll cut off one of Sonja's finger and send it as a souvenir!"

One of the detectives got suspicious about the note and told Emily she needed to go to the police station with him to give writing samples. The other detectives searched the whole house again and found the gun she had said the intruder had pointed at her. Everything looked strange to the detectives. I was too upset to be suspicious, and my mind played all kind of tricks on me, showing me Sonja in some ditch screaming for me; her finger coming to the house in an envelope; her being hungry, scared, and crying for her mama, tied to a chair. The waiting drove me up the wall, the uncertainty, the worry, and the helplessness. Emily was brought back to the house. Five long hours of hoping and praying had gone by without a sign, when the detectives took me to the side and told me that they had a suspicion and we all needed to go to the police station.

In the car on the way to the police station, Emily started crying again and said how sorry she felt for me and that she would pray that Sonja came back safe. Some detectives stayed at the house, and the ones at the police station made me look at a big book with pictures of criminals to see if I had seen anyone before. The police had taken Emily to another room, and after two hours of questioning her, she finally broke down and admitted that she and a friend of hers had come up with the idea of kidnapping Sonja. She would not say where Sonja was until she would board an airplane back to Birmingham, Alabama.

We were on the way to the airport when I just looked at her and could not believe that she did something like this. I wanted so badly to hurt her the way she had hurt me, but one detective must have seen how I felt and kept holding my hands. He said, "Don't do it; she isn't worth it!" Everything had been arranged, and at 11:00 p.m. when she got into the airplane, she finally told us that Sonja was in a day and night care center and gave us the address. The airplane took off, and at 11:45 p.m. my eight-plus-hour nightmare came to an end when I could hold my little girl in my arms again. She did not even know what was going on. She had been told that Mama had to go and do some Christmas shopping. The police told me that Emily had told them that she thought she deserved some of John's insurance money since she had an affair with him and had taken care of Sonja when she was being held in Alabama. The irony of it all was that there was no insurance money, since John had stopped making payments six months before his death.

I was very angry and asked if she would get away with kidnapping but was told that the paperwork had to be finished, a court hearing had to be arranged, and then they would get her back to Texas for the trial. I could not believe that someone who had received only good things from me could do such a thing. She came without money, and I supported her, helped her look for work, and I thought we had a good relationship. My trust in humankind was, as so often before, destroyed once more. Only someone with children of their own can imagine the torture these hours brought to me. I swore again I would not help anyone anymore, but deep in my heart I knew better.

Time went by with me driving the school bus and going to finish my GED. At the beginning of the next year I was summoned to the courthouse to tell what had happened on the day of the kidnapping. Emily had been picked up in Alabama and brought back to Texas to stand trial. She had thought she was home free after leaving Texas. Confronted with her family, I told it like it happened. They gave me some dirty looks, but I ignored them. The judge's verdict confined her to a Texas jail for three months, and back in Alabama, she had to participate in a work program for nine months. It was her first offense. That is why, I guess, she got away with a light sentence. I hoped that later in life, when she had children of her own, she would realize what she had put me through. When questioned, she never revealed the name of her helper in committing the crime.

After she had left, life went on slow and easy, and my concentration went to Sonja and my future. Driving a bus was not something I would like to do for the rest of my life. Right now it was convenient to take Sonja with me and not have to pay for a babysitter. Every time I looked at her, I was thankful that she was unharmed and did not even know that she had been kidnapped again. She was a happy child, and all my love went to her, trying to make her forget that her daddy never would come back. Often she asked, "Where is Daddy?" and my answer was always "In your heart, sweetheart, in the trees, in the sun, and in the sky!"

Another step toward my future was accomplished when, in March 1977, I received my GED certificate. Now I started looking into the possibilities of higher education. John had started courses once, under the army's GI Bill, to become an air conditioning and heating repairman, but gave up after two months. I had driven to Austin with Sonja several times and looked around for universities, since there was only the small Central Texas College in Killeen that offered only two years of education. I was looking for a university that offered bachelor programs. I liked St. Edward's University at first sight, and after finding out that I could use the GI bill for my studies, I came to the decision to move to Austin with Sonja. We found a house close to St. Edward's and a kindergarten for Sonja, and in the fall I enrolled in St. Edward's.

The time Sonja was in kindergarten I spent in school. It was very hard, but I enjoyed it very much. As I fought with the English language and tried to do the very best I could, the years at St. Edward's became the best years of my life. It was up to me to be the best, and with the help of a very caring faculty, I kept an almost perfect grade point average. The only problem was that I could not decide what subject I wanted to concentrate on. Everything was fascinating to me, and I wanted to know something about everything. I loved art but was often discouraged by the talent of others and told myself that there would be no future in it for my child or me. Brother Hilarion, my art professor, had a different opinion, but just the fact that most artists become famous only after their death made me pursue different subjects. Over the years I found out that learning itself was the most loved subject for me. I loved learning about Emerson, Thoreau, Hawthorne, Monet, Picasso, Van Gogh, marketing, accounting, biology, and a variety of other subjects.

Two years of studies were behind me when I planed a vacation for both of us. Over the years, I had kept in contact with my half sister in Berlin. She had remarried and had two little girls, about the same age as Sonja. She and her new husband had a bar and worked late hours, drinking a lot and living a hectic life. The constant drinking had turned her husband into an alcoholic, and every now and then he tried to get out of the cycle, which resulted in seizures and hospital stays. In 1979, we had planned on a visit to Berlin, but shortly before our scheduled departure, I received news of his death. During a stay in the hospital, he had bitten off his tongue during a seizure and choked to death on it. Our supposed vacation visit ended up being a funeral visit.

why she left them for
ve anything to do with
I wanted to get to know
pinion about them, she
r she would never talk

nths while she was in
difficult month in my
ike around her; then a
s hard. My guilt about
ng with my wondering
with her and she would
were questions no one
ent outbreaks, swear
hings, and misunder
gh to come to a ground
Her favorite song she
r crying into her room
is, I want you to show
wledge that we needed
rter and grow together
d with time we would
ecome friends.
e the anger in her and
hought was in her hea
er to my half sister and
out not knowing that
parately and in homes
d, being used as work
her that there were
which no one had any
did not help anything.

A TRIP TO BERLIN

After almost twenty hours traveling (I made the mistake of letting Sonja convince me to take the train from Frankfurt to Berlin, since she had never been on a train) we finally made it to Berlin. Because Sonja was nine years old and had no knowledge of the German language, I was worried at first about her being bored, and not getting along with my sister's two children. I was amazed at how well the children got along; language seemed very unimportant. All three in the same age group, they communicated with hands and feet and had a wonderful time. Seeing how well they played together and how well the two of us understood each other, my sister started ganging up on me, wanting me to move back to Germany, to be together, to have the children grow up together. We could finally have what neither of us had: a family.

She was so sad about her husband because she had loved him very much. The funeral was sad, and she depended on me for the weeks to come to take care of the children and the house. She really wanted for us to be together. We got to know each other better now and seemed to get along just fine. My secret wishes of knowing where I belonged, having people I could trust, having family, surfaced again. I promised to think about it and let her know soon enough to find a place for us in case we really wanted to come to Berlin. We enjoyed our time together, including the zoo visits, the beautiful Berlin surrounding, the Grunewald, the Charlottenburger Schloss, the museums, and even the depressing visits to the border and to the memorial museum at Checkpoint Charlie, which showed the history of the border and all the different ways people invented to escape it. Chills went over my spine thinking back how I had escaped from the East. Pictures in the museum showed how people had rebuilt the trunks of cars to accommodate a person, homemade air balloons, underground tunnels, secret compartments added to cars, and a cable used to rail people from one house to the other over the border out of the communist part of Berlin. Most of these escape attempts were stopped later when houses along the border were destroyed and the place between East and West was extended to make room for a mile-wide death strip with mines, control towers, barbed wire, watchdogs, and the ten-foot-high border. Many lost their lives in attempts to escape, and the rest, locked in, gave up, and had to learn to survive.

DECISIONS, DECISIONS

Our vacation had come to an end, and back in America I had one year to make up my mind if I should start all over again in Germany. Another fact became very important. Gloria, my first daughter, had turned eighteen, and I know that the people who adopted her had to tell her about it. I had kept in touch with the adoption agency and started looking for her. From the agency I found out that she had left her adoptive parents and had moved to Mainz on the Rhein River. At the same time, she had started looking for me, but she did not have my social security number and could not find me. The German system, of having to report to the police and leave a forwarding address, helped me to find out her address, and soon I wrote a long letter to her.

The urge to belong and the possibility of seeing Gloria again, since it would be a lot easier for her to come to Berlin than to America, also played a role in my decision to return to Germany. My sister's letters sounded very loving and encouraging and convinced me I was doing the right thing. Making friends was very hard for me in America, and since my sister was by herself also, I thought everything should be a lot easier for two sisters with children. If all else failed, I could still come back to

America. After I had made the decision, the rest came easy: selling everything, buying airplane tickets, and getting passports ...

A NEW START

After thirteen hours of flying, we arrived in Berlin in July, 1980. My sister had known for four months now that we were coming, but to my great disappointment, she had not even looked for an apartment for us. So we had to stay with her until I found a job and an apartment. Till then I became the built-in babysitter, cook, maid, and taxi driver. She had never been by herself before and had to find out what life is all about (after five children). I understood her longing to experience life for the first time without rules and constraints. After a while I tried to talk some sense into her, tried to make her stop bringing men home and letting her children see her drunk. Many times she called me from some bar to pick her up, but when I got there she needed one more drink, and one more, and I was sitting and waiting until she was ready to be driven home. The bars did not close in Berlin. That was something I did not know, and being called at three or five in the morning was not my idea of having fun.

That was not what I had expected from her and we had many bad discussions about it. Since I had developed into such a party pooper, she soon found another woman who felt the same way she did, and they became very good friends. At least I was relieved of playing taxi driver for my drunken sister. Often I asked her why she wanted me here and what had happened to the nice ideas in her letters about being together, doing things together with the children, and getting to know each other a lot better.

After a long search I finally found a job with an insurance company, managing four apartment houses in Neukölln. With the job came an apartment, with two bedrooms, and one bath. I was happy to have my own place again and to be thirty minutes away from my sister. We needed space between us. For Sonja I found a Baptist school, since she could not speak German. I was happy that the next year a place became available in the John F. Kennedy School, a school that taught in German and English. The bad part was that it was a forty-minute commute by subway and bus. The transit system in Berlin was out of this world; a car was unnecessary but still very desirable just for the convenience of not having to carry groceries in the subway or bus.

Sonja had to learn fast which buses to take to get to school and come home. She was ten years old now, and having German children around her taught her the German language very quickly. Nevertheless, the first year was very hard for her because she greatly missed Stacia, her best friend from Austin. I was busy turning an apartment into a home again, buying furniture and small things, and working almost twelve hours a day. Tenants always had questions, emergencies arose after hours, and snow and ice had to be taken care of early in the morning and late in the evening. Otherwise life was pretty good. We were healthy, had a nice home, and every now and then met with my sister.

To my amazement I suddenly had an aunt and uncle

also, who lived almost around the corner from us. I found out that at the time I needed a helping hand, when I first came to Berlin, neither of them wanted to have anything to do with either of my real mother's children. Now I was suddenly introduced to two strangers and had to call them aunt and uncle; it was quite hard and puzzling for me. Soon I found that having a family had its ups and downs. Guilt and blame were pushed around from one to another, leaving me with the sense of wondering and mistrust. The loving, helping, and understanding among us had yet to be found.

The relationship among all of us became a little better, but the circumstances for Sonja had gotten worse. She was eleven now and had to get up every morning at 6:00 a.m. and come home at 6:00 p.m., just like a grownup. She had to change from the bus to the subway to the American school bus to get to school in Grunewald. Her health started to deteriorate and a doctor told me that this schedule was just too much for her, and that we needed to get closer to the school. Searching for another job closer to Grunewald, I found another position managing just one building with a beautiful three-bedroom, one-bath apartment. Sonja just had to walk five minutes to the American school bus stop, and my work was cut in half with the same pay. God took care of us again. Soon I also started working for the German post office, sorting mail from 4:00 to 8:00 a.m. My sister had found a new job also just around the corner from me, and we started getting along a lot better.

The children played together after school, and every now and then, we visited our aunt and uncle. Our aunt soon came to be known by the children as the "five-Mark aunt" (she gave the children five Marks, about three dollars) every time they came to visit. None of us were very crazy about visiting them, since we had to ride the bus and subway forty-five minutes to get there. Another disliked chore: they lived on the fourth floor, with no elevator and no central heating. In the wintertime one of us had to carry coal and wood from the cellar up the four flights so that they could heat the apartment. We offered to go run errands for them, and soon it became expected that we did it. One of us was expected to clean the windows and the apartment, and once, after my uncle had died, I renovated the whole apartment (wallpapered, painted, lowered the ceiling in the hall, installed lighting, and laid new carpet).

The more we both did for them, the more they expected of us. When we could not go sometimes, we were asked from Switzerland, by our real mother, why we did not go and help. "They are old people and need your help." It amazed me repeatedly how people who did not wanted anything to do with us when we were younger now took it for granted to be there for them, nurturing and helping them. When asked why they avoided us when we were younger, they used their new business they had just started as an excuse. It required all the attention they could give and did not leave time for anything else.

FINDING LOVE AGAIN AND GLORIA

My sister and I went out together sometimes. On one of these occasions, we got to know Roman, who seemed very interested in me. He was tall, had dark blond hair, and had very pretty dark eyes, which seemed to be able to look to the bottom of your soul. He took care of his appearance and had beautiful hands (I was always fascinated by hands). After we met several times, we started going out together. The second time in my life that someone brought me flowers, paid attention to me, and liked to dance with me. He was a warm, intelligent, romantic and interesting man for about four months until the real Roman appeared. Having waited an hour for him one day, I gave up and went home to wait another three days before I heard from him again. He admitted that he had a problem—drinking. Every three to four months, it would hit him, and he could not control himself. He had to drink until he could not remember who he was and where he was. He told me he woke up several times in places he could not remember how he got there. He hated it, but he could not stop. He did not want to join any Alcohol Anonymous group because he thought, from one time to another, that he could control it. When he was sober we could talk for hours; he knew something about everything. He was very nice and loving to Sonja and a gentleman to me, the ideal partner, until the third or fourth month came along. I really loved him and was under the impression that if I would stand by him, support and help him, he would get over it and stop. Months went by; the periods between drinking became longer, but then they became shorter again. I hated the times when he dragged himself home, drunk, waking Sonja and me. I tried patience, forgiving, love, understanding, hate, but after almost two years of trying, I had to give it up. I realized that all of it was in vain since he did not agree to get help. He just was too proud to admit to himself that he needed help. To have a young girl grow up under such circumstances was not my idea of a good environment. Since we were not married, I could call it off. The distance between us helped, since he had an apartment in Wilmersdorf and we lived in Grunewald, but I needed a long time to get over him. I kept asking myself, "What else could I have expected to find in a bar?" and swore not to get caught up again in dreams about finding a good man.

Soon I found myself unfulfilled again and turned to studies again, attending the University of Maryland (European Division) in Berlin.

GLORIA

I had kept in contact with Gloria through letters, and one day I got a letter saying that she would like to come and visit for while to get to know her real mother and her half sister. Sonja and I were very nervous when we stood at the gate at the Tegel airport to pick her up. I had no idea what she looked like; I did not have a picture, nothing. People came out and I concentrated only on girls around the twenties, traveling alone. There she was—it could only be her! Dark hair, brown eyes, and of small stature, she reminded me of Rolf right away. She looked at me and Sonja, asking, "Mutti?" and we were in each other's arms, crying, hugging, and forgetting all about Sonja and everyone else. Slowly letting go, I introduced Sonja to Gloria. The short "hello" should have made me realize what lay ahead for us.

Back in the apartment, I showed her the room I had prepared for her. It was a small bedroom. Sonja had the bigger one, and that was the first thing Gloria did not like. She would have liked if I had put Sonja in the little bedroom. She felt like a guest, but she was also my daughter, I was told. I did not say anything. We went and did a lot of things together, and I tried to make her stay as pleasant and memorable as possible. Nothing seemed to please her, and I got to know a very egocentric, insecure, and troubled young woman. If she caught me giving Sonja a hug or good night kisses, she got very upset and told me, "You love Sonja more than me because she's prettier than me."

She admitted that she had had all the material things a child could have wished for, that her adoptive parents did a lot financially for her, but that they could not give her love. They had bought her a horse and paid for her higher education, guitar and dance lessons, and vacations. When I ask why she left them, she told me that she had come home late one night and gotten a slap in the face from her mother. That is why she left them for good and never ever wanted to have anything to do with them anymore. When I told her I wanted to get to know them to be able to form my own opinion about them, she exploded and told me if I did that she would never talk to me again.

Needless to say, the three months while she was in Berlin became some of the most difficult month in my life. Everything and all had to revolve around her; then it was fine, and she was happy. It was hard. My guilt about giving her away was renewed, along with my wondering if somehow I could have made it with her and she would not have been so mixed up. These were questions no one could answer. A lot of tears, hysteric outbreaks, swearing of love, missed kisses, missed hugs, and misunderstandings had to be worked through to come to a ground we both could communicate on. Her favorite song she played when she was angry and run crying into her room was "I want to know what love is, I want you to show me." We finally came to the knowledge that we needed time to get to know each other better and grow together. We knew that we were related and with time we would find a basis to relate and maybe become friends.

She needed to learn to resolve the anger in her and to understand that I did what I thought was in her best interest at the time. I introduced her to my half sister and her children, along with our story about not knowing that we had each other, growing up separately and in homes where love was an unknown word, being used as working machines. We all tried to show her that there were circumstances in all our lives over which no one had any control and that living in the past did not help anything.

It is what you make out of your life and out of yourself that counts. We thought if we made her realize that the hard life we had did not leave us very many opportunities and choices, she would understand the "Why?" she asked so often.

When we took her to the airport, neither of us had any tears, and we said goodbye with the promise to think about everything and write to each other. Sonja, at first excited to have her own sister, was also happy after Gloria had left and life returned to the old routine.

Gloria's visit revived a question that was bothering me for quite a while: "Why did my foster mother do the things she did to me?"

ave him and me alone.
sat down and told me
estions. I told him that
ure to answer all of his
I could explain how I
though I was born in
become an American
for a number of years
ring in the army. I told
if he were still in the
and that my husband
I had a lot of contacts
everywhere on the
A and in the commu
doing. After a while I
nswered enough ques-
me again, and I asked
night have some more
him again. He told me
ter he had left, we dis-
hus told me that if I
n and keep him happy.
s. Wanda said the next
stay with me. All of us
eally wanted and how

of weeks had gone by
was that man. I was
from where he got my
wered, "We have
nd put the paperwork
that he wanted to meet

A VISIT INTO THE PAST

As an American citizen, I could travel to the East of Germany now without being stopped. Nevertheless, I still wanted to find out in advance if it really was safe to go with Sonja for a visit since I had escaped. Inquiries were made, and I was told that the East Germans could not do anything to my daughter or me, since we were Americans, and just to follow their rules by not importing anything that was forbidden. All food items were allowed. We would have to exchange West currency into East German from the East German police to enter for the days of stay, and avoid importing anything that had West German propaganda in it (including magazines, war toys, weapons, books, and extra West German currency).

I wanted Sonja to see how I grew up and where I went to school and to meet my foster mother. She told me that she was afraid to meet my foster mother after all the things I had told her, but I quieted her down by telling her I would be there and I would take care of her. I remembered what things were always welcome to bring, what was very expensive for the East German people to buy, and what they liked: coffee, chocolate, nylons, fruits, and many other items, most of them considered luxuries by the East German government.

So one day, loaded with goodies, we got in the car and drove toward East Germany. As Americans we had to enter and exit the East at the Checkpoint Charlie (for foreign travelers), an opening in the border in Neukölln. The closer we got, the more doubts I had about whether this was the right thing to do, putting us both in danger. But I also saw it as putting an end to a lot of questions in my mind. In addition, I also wanted to find out what had happened to Wanda, my best friend from school. How Mittenwalde had changed, who had married whom, and how living was in the East compared to the West.

There was a short stop at Checkpoint Charlie with a look at our passports, and then the East German border patrol. We had to leave the car, exchange our West currency for East currency (25.00 West German Marks per day for 25.00 East German Marks, which looked, by the way, like monopoly money). Sonja was too young to have to pay. Our car was put into a special garage and searched inside and out, and I had to go into a room where a policewoman came and searched me. All the time I was wondering and worried if they had kept a list of all the people who had escaped the DDR and if they would tell me the next minute that they had been waiting for me and put me in jail. Trembling inside, trying to be calm, I was finally, after thirty minutes, reunited with Sonja. I had answered all their questions about why I wanted to go to the East, what I wanted to do there, and what amount of money I was bringing in.

Having been instructed not to make extra stops on the way, we were ready to go. After forty-five minutes of driving through unfamiliar areas, watching my speed limit and all traffic signs carefully, we came to a surrounding familiar to me: Mittenwalde. The old bridge leading over a small river looked even older, the streets looked like as they looked in 1950, the houses looked a lot smaller, and a lot more run down, and all seemed as if the city had been asleep for twenty years. I had come in an American car (a 1974 Buick Rivera), which had caused already some excitement on the way when a man riding a bicycle, looking at the car and not watching where he was going, had run into an electrical pole. In the little village, the excitement was even greater. People came outside to look at the car, children ran around it with "oohs" and "aahs," and people opened windows to see what was going on. Barely out of the car, holding presents, Sonja and me had women walking up to us, asking where we were going, and whom we were visiting. When I told them Heather, they said right away, "You must be Barbara," and that they had heard that we were coming (*From whom?* I was wondering).

The house had not changed at all, and when I opened the front door, a cold chill went over my back. After all these years, I was still afraid. I kept telling myself that I was a grown woman now with children of my own, and I did not need to be afraid anymore. Climbing the stairs to Heather's rooms brought back a lot of memories. I knocked on the door. No response. I opened the door and just went in, and I saw Heather sitting in a chair at the window looking outside. She looked at me and said she could not get up, her legs hurt too much. She said we should sit down and asked if I could make her some coffee. I unpacked the presents I had brought, and she could suddenly get up and put them right away out of sight. She said, "You can't let others see what you got, they get jealous." Sonja was hiding behind me, and Heather told her to come to her and say hi. She did and came right back to me.

We went to the kitchen where absolutely nothing had changed, cooked us coffee, and ate the cake I had brought. We talked a lot, and she told me that she was sure I would show up one day. I wanted to know what had happened to Wanda, my next door neighbor friend I had played with for years. She told me she did not know where she went, that she lost sight of her. I knew that in a little town like this everybody knew what was going on, and what happened to everyone. Finally, I came out with the question for which I came: "Why all the beatings, the hunger, the nights on my knees on the floor in front of the bed, the cellar with the rats, and the constant working, working?" "To turn you into a good human being" was the answer. The other question I wanted answered was, "Why had she taken me? She had obviously never loved me." She answered, so that she would have someone who would take care of her when she grew old. We did not stay very long, I needed to get out. With a promise to return, we left and drove around Mittenwalde, showing Sonja where I had to collect horse manure, where the garden was that I had to work in as a child, where I had to get milk, and where I went to school. At the school, we got out of the car and went inside. I told Sonja, "Your mother went up and down these stairs, and she sat and learned in these classrooms." Suddenly, a man approached us asking us what we were doing here. I told him I was from America and just wanted to show my daughter where I used to go to school. He told us we could not do this, it was forbidden for anyone not belonging to the school to just come walking in and look.

We left, and after showing Sonja the lake where I used to swim and the mountain where we used to listen to West German music, I drove back to Checkpoint Charlie, tired and shocked. We were searched again, and when we got to the West part of Berlin, a big relief came over us. We decided to wait a while before going back, but I still wanted to find out what had happened to the other children from my school, and especially Wanda. After two more visits, I convinced Heather to come with me to Königs Wusterhausen where Wanda's parents had a car shop. Wanda had shown me where her parents lived, and I remembered that it was not far from the main train station in Königs Wusterhausen. Since not much had changed in Mittenwalde, I hoped that the same was true of Königs Wusterhausen.

The drive to Königs Wusterhausen brought back memories of the good kind. I had loved riding my bicycle through the nice landscape, and all was exactly as I remembered. Heather asked, "Remember the Hoffmanns, the Kellers, the Schönemanns? Karl had married Lisa; Jürgen had married Jutta." Most of the names I heard did not sound familiar anymore. I had forgotten most of them. When coming into Königs Wusterhausen, I was shocked again—just like in Mittenwalde, time had stood still for twenty years. All the buildings looked run down. When I reached the house where Wanda's parents had their car shop, I parked, went in, and asked where I could find Wanda. I was told that Wanda went shopping, so I left a message that "Barbara from Texas is here to see her and is waiting for her in the restaurant by the main train station." She told me later that she thought someone was trying to make a fool out of her, but she was still curious to find out.

Heather, Sonja, and I were sitting at the restaurant eating that good German cake, drinking coffee, and waiting for Wanda, when a car pulled up. After twenty-five years, I saw Wanda again! I knew right away that it was Wanda. The face had not changed much, even though she had gotten pretty big. She looked at me, then at Heather, and made the connection right away. We hugged, laughed, cried, and could not believe that we had found each other again. There was a lot to talk about and not enough time, so we promised to stay in contact. I had to promise to come back and visit and meet her family. She was married and had a son about ten years older than Sonja. With her I had found the kind of welcome I had hoped for from my "family." We took Heather back to Mittenwalde and left to return to West Berlin.

Sonja liked Wanda right away and wanted to go back to see her again. Back in Berlin we stayed in touch with Wanda, I wrote her, and she wrote back, inviting us again and again. We went to her husband's birthday party, loaded down with presents, and were happy to see a nice house on the lake they had built almost by themselves. A small bungalow next to the lake was ready for us to stay in for several days. Wanda had baked pies and cakes and cooked up food for at least twenty people. Many came to celebrate the birthday. I could see right away that the family was very popular around Niederlehme, a suburb about twenty minutes from Königs Wusterhausen. They had bought the property from Wanda's parents and had built the house on it. Two sailboats were parked on the grass, along with two cars, and I thought times could not be as bad as they were said to be. I got to know their son, a tall young man with a warm smile, intelligent, knowing exactly what he can and cannot expect from the future. He knew he would have to join the East German army very soon, which was mandatory. He had a girlfriend in Kamenz, a three-hour drive from his house, and he loved to talk, sail, collect stamps, and coins from other countries. At the birthday party, I got to know their friends and how the people partied in the East: until four or five in the morning, with a lot of alcohol, laughter, dancing, music, and grilling. We enjoyed the time very much, and I could have conversations with her husband like I used to have with Roman. Klaus, six feet five inches tall, blond hair, and a big beard covering half of his face, blue eyes, he looked like a captain from a big ship. He liked to talk, was very intelligent, liked to laugh, and liked to hear from me what was going on outside the DDR and in America.

Slowly, I found out how everything worked now in the East. I was very interested and Klaus never got tired of talking about it and answering my questions. He told me that they had to register Rudolph (their son) at a local civil office when he was born in order that he could get his driver's license when he turned eighteen and get a car by then. Just going out and just buying one was impossible. The DDR (German Democratic Republic) produced only two kinds of cars: the Borgward, and the Trabant (the Trabant was a two-cylinder car with a maximum of fifty miles per hour speed). A twenty-year wait was normal to get a new car, so people were forced to keep their cars in good shape as long as possible. Credit cards, what are those? Get a loan? No way. Money had to be saved so that in case something became available you had the money to buy it.

Whatever was produced in the DDR was exported right away, leaving very few articles for the public! The East German currency was not welcomed in the West, only in other communist countries, so exporting was the only (besides visitation rights, and popular singers being sent to the West) way to get West currency. Everything that did not grow in the East, for example bananas, oranges, and kiwis, was only available twice a year, and then you had to drive forty-five minutes to East Berlin to get it. If you were lucky, they would still have some when you finally made it there, but most of the time you had to stay in line for an hour, and when you got to the front of the line it was: "Sorry, we are all out." The same thing could happen to you when going to the butcher shop, the clothing store, and the electrical appliance store. If a television was offered for 800 Deutsche Marks in West Berlin, the same television had a sales tag of 3000 East Marks! All items that were considered luxury by the government were extremely expensive. The income of a regular worker in the East was about 400 East Marks a month. On the other hand, living was very cheap. An apartment went for 25 to 75 East Marks a month. Groceries were quite inexpensive, but not always available. Because of the low rents, housing could not be repaired. Material for repairs was very hard to come by. That was the reason why everything looked so run down. Klaus told me also that he had been successful so far in not having to join the East German party since he had his own business. It was mandatory (in an employee employer situation), if you wanted to succeed and get ahead, that you had to enter the Socialistic Unity Party of the East German government. It was a common saying in the West that everyone in the East with a house, two cars, and sailboats must be in the party, but Wanda and Klaus were not.

Klaus's company built and repaired trailers for big trucks, receiving his contracts from the government. He said business was good enough to get by, and with wheeling and dealing they even got enough together to build the house and make a good living. Connections were absolutely necessary in order to find out when and where needed supplies were available. Then they had to have the ability to drop everything and have the necessary money supply available to buy. If you are employed in a regular eight-to-five job and without connections or friends, it will usually be too late. The weekends were building and repair time. Most East Germans rented a little piece of land with a little weekend house on it close to the lake and grew their own vegetables and fruits. This way they knew they would have what they needed. The beer and hard liquor for parties were cheap and the food was home cooked and not of great variety, but the people and the landscape made up for many shortcomings. Another thing had not changed in all the years. Listening to West channels on TV and radio was still forbidden, and people still approached those they did not know with suspicion. They did not say anything against the government around such people. The next door neighbor could be a spy for the STASI (State Security Police).

We enjoyed the lakes around Wanda's home. The little bungalow was always ready for us when we came to visit, and conversations were always interesting. Even though their time was filled with working, they still made time for us to eat lunch, have time in the midafternoon (about 3:00 p.m.) for coffee, homemade cakes, and baked goods (Wanda baked the best pies and cakes). Tables by the lake always turned these hours into special events. Neighbors came to participate in a game of volleyball or just sit and have a drink or some barbeque with us. The neighbor did a lot of fishing and often gave some fish to Wanda and Klaus, who prepared them over an open fire. All in all, this was good living in pleasant company.

After his mandatory army interval, their son studied in Leipzig to become an engineer like his father. Wanda had managed a day care center before she started to run the administrative part of their business. All were, to a certain extent, satisfied with their lives, complaining only about not being able to travel outside communist areas, and having always to wheel and deal to get what was wanted and needed. I helped them get the things they needed for the house from the West, and all of us enjoyed each other's company. When we visited we usually stayed two to five days, always stopping by Heather's with presents. I got used to that most of the times I had to go to the visits by myself because Sonja did not like Heather and would rather stay at Wanda's house.

SPY FOR US

After we had gone to visit several times, Wanda met us one day on the border all excited. She was very upset, and we sat down in the car so that she could tell me what was going on. She told me that they had had a visitor from the STASI who wanted to know about their guests from the West. He had told Wanda that he would be there when I visited the next time. He had asked questions over questions about how it could be that I was born in the East but was an American, and whether I could still shop in the US soldiers' shopping center, if I could still go on post, and so on. Wanda had only answered she did not know and that he would have to ask me. Wanda cried and told me she felt so angry and ashamed that they would not leave her guests alone. I calmed her down and told her not to worry, that they could not touch us and I would talk to the guy. When we got to her house, about twenty minutes later, someone knocked on the front door.

A man, flashing a badge no one could read so fast, not introducing himself, looked around and walked toward the dining table. Average looking, nothing that would catch your eye, he mentioned that he was from the STASI. His sharp, dark, piercing eyes looked me over with a short glance. His dark suit looked like it had seen better times. He told Wanda to leave him and me alone. Wanda took Sonja and left. He sat down and told me that he needed to ask me some questions. I told him that he could ask, but I could not promise to answer all of his questions. He started by asking if I could explain how I became an American citizen even though I was born in Mittenwalde. I told him that I had become an American citizen and had lived in America for a number of years. He asked what my husband was doing in the army. I told him that I would not be sitting here if he were still in the army, he should know that himself, and that my husband died. Next he wanted to know if I had a lot of contacts with Americans, if I could go freely everywhere on the army post, if I could shop in the PX and in the commissary, and what kind of work I was doing. After a while I had enough and told him I had answered enough questions. He asked if he could meet me again, and I asked him what for? He said that he might have some more questions. I asked if I had to meet him again. He told me it would be in my best interest. After he had left, we discussed everything, and Wanda and Klaus told me that if I would not meet with the man again and keep him happy, he could make trouble for all of us. Wanda said the next time she would come with me and stay with me. All of us were interested to know what he really wanted and how far he would go.

Back in the West, a couple of weeks had gone by when I received a telephone call. It was that man. I was stunned that I asked right away from where he got my telephone number. He just answered, "We have our ways!" He told me he knew that I had put the paperwork in for another visa to visit and that he wanted to meet me on the way to Wanda's at the entrance of the youth camp I always had to pass. After he had hung up, I called Wanda, and she told me she would be there to stick by my side. We met there, and about ten minutes later, that man showed up. He told Wanda that he wanted to talk to me alone. I told him whatever he had to say Wanda could hear. He started throwing out hints about how expensive everything was and that Sonja and I would not have to exchange any money anymore at the border and could even earn West money if I could help him to find out certain things about the West and the Americans. I looked at him and asked him what I was supposed to find out for him. He told me he would let me know. He also wanted to meet again in East Berlin at the Alexander Platz Rathaus (restaurant) for dinner, at which time he would let me know.

We had heated conversations about what they could do if I did not cooperate with him. Wanda and Klaus felt very helpless because they realized they could not do anything to stop him from bothering me or them. I assured them I would find out, once back in the West, what I could do. At home again, I made several phone calls and found out that there was a special office in Berlin I would have to go to and report the incident. I also would have to report to the American authorities. I just had found out about this and hang up the phone, when it was ringing again. He was on the phone telling me to meet him at the restaurant. Angry, I agreed, wanting to tell him right to his face that I would report him and he had better stop calling and bothering my friends and me.

When I met him two days later, I told him to leave my friends and me alone or that I would report him to the authorities. He just looked at me and said, "I do not know what anyone could have against making good money just for a little information!" I said that I could tell him the temperature in Berlin if he wanted to pay me for that. He laughed and said, "No we just want information about how many Americans are stationed in Berlin, where they are located, what weapons they have, where they have their maneuvers, and whether I could get in contact with certain people."

I looked at him and asked, "What if I do not go along with you? Can you stop me from visiting my friends?"

He said clearly, "Yes!" and pointed out that I was from the East and had grown up here, so I should be willing to help my home country.

I retorted, "That is exactly why I never would help the STASI or anyone connected with it because I saw how it was, and I see how it still is. The same people you want me to get information for fired shots at me when the only thing I wanted was to be free. Don't you think you are asking the impossible?" I got up and left him sitting there, knowing he could stop me if he wanted to. I had talked loud enough that other people in the restaurant could understand me and I hoped that this was the reason that he didn't follow me. My heart was racing all the way until I got home.

The next morning I went straight to the German agency called Border Relations and told them about what happened. Everything was written down, and I was asked to describe the man. Only then did I realize that I could not find anything special about him. He had no birthmark, no long nose, no special height, nor unusual clothing, nor had he any points of interest at all. He was a truly inconspicuous human being and hard to describe. I was told that this was the way the STASI operated, that they pick such people on purpose to recruit spies for them. After leaving the German agency, I went to the American agency on post and reported everything that had happened. I wanted to know if I really could run into problems if I decided to visit my friends again. They told me to let about six months pass and after that it should be all right to visit again. They advised that, should I be approached again, I should let the man know that I had reported him and not talk to him anymore after that. Every future contact would have to be reported.

I wrote my friends about everything, and Wanda called me shortly after that, telling me just to go along with it, and she needed to talk to me when I could visit again. After six months went by, I had called the American agency to find out if they thought it was safe for us to visit again. They said it would be all right and gave me a telephone number to call should I run into any problems. With butterflies in my stomach, I drove to the Checkpoint Charlie. When I had to look into the border guard's face so he could compare my face to the picture on my passport, and when I was searched again, I asked myself, *Why am I doing this, putting Sonja and myself through this?* I answered myself, *To prove that no one can put any restraints on my daughter or on me anymore. We are Americans, and we will not be restricted in our freedom to go where we want to go and see whom we want to see.* Finally, after one hour, we were released and could go. Driving through the countryside, I had to be very careful not to speed and to follow the street signs. The East German police were known for stopping West cars to collect West currency, and West cars were easy to spot. Very few times did we see a West car with East license plates on it, and we knew right away that a relative had bought the car in the West and given it as a present. The East German government officials usually drove cars like Mercedes and Volvos. They wanted to

After we arrived at Wanda's house, we sat down and caught up on the latest news. She had found out that her next door neighbor had told on them about having frequent visits from the West. Jealousy about their having nice things and getting what they needed through me played a big role in it. She told me that before having visits from certain people, she had to hide several things in the house to avoid jealousy. She had only a few friends, whom she had known for a very long time and thought that she could trust. She never had any contact with the next-door neighbor since she knew that he worked for the STASI. I asked her if she had heard from the man after I had reported him. She said he had called her and told her he would stop me from seeing her, and when she asked, "How?" he had answered, "I'll find a way!" She told me he sounded angry. We were worried that he might appear again at Wanda's house, but he stayed away. After several visits we started to forget about the attempts to hire me as a spy and enjoyed each other's company again. Sonja enjoyed fishing with Wanda's son and the neighbor children, going swimming, picking mushrooms, and eating Wanda's good cooking. Often we said it would be nice if I could invite them to visit us too, if only Wanda could just get into her car and surprise me with a visit.

We shared these longings with a lot of people. Most of them had their lives settled; some of them also had their own businesses. They did not even want to leave their homes or their businesses. It just would have meant so much if they could have gone to visit or shop in the West and come home again. Wanda and Klaus had experienced the time before the border and could remember the ease of getting merchandise and "luxury" goods in the West, but their son did not know how it was before, and that things could be a lot better. His parents gave him the opportunity to travel to Russia and Czechoslovakia, and trips all over East Germany. When he got home again he helped his parents in the business. Their afternoon coffee breaks, visits to friends and family, sailing, grilling, playing softball, and other leisure time activities would soon be, to everyone's surprise, reduced almost to nonexistence.

discontentment. Youth
e Skinheads, used this
ot and indulge in dis
rnment for unemploy-
heir freedom of expres-
ad been an exclusive
rants, and shops, soon
ans and rebel marches.
down to condemned
e working class lived
ple so why not use it.
ets or cardboard, graf
condemning the West
work and housing. A
their domain, with
ght.

the fall of the bo
ks, rented student, to
ny people to look fo

nexistent ties with th
layed a big role in my
back to America. Fo
xpected by anyone.

DOUBTS AND RUMORS

Our lives were running smoothly. Sonja was doing well in the German American school, her German had improved, she had new friends, and she liked being with her cousins. Every now and then my sister and I went out dancing, drinking, and just having fun. I had learned not to wait for her anymore. When I got tired, I just told her I was going home and she had to take a taxi. I managed apartments now for several years already and still worked from four to eight in the morning at the post office. The relationship with my sister was sometimes a loving one, and other times we did not talk to each other for years in a row. The same was true about my real mother. The causes were mostly jealousy, gossip, and favoritism. I was astounded when my mother and her husband came to visit. The people, who had not raised us and were never there for us, were suddenly under the impression when they came to visit that we had to wait on them from morning to night. The same was true for my aunt (whom I only got to know since I came back to Germany). Things were taken for granted, for instance running errands, planting and watering my uncle's grave, going shopping, etc. Whoever did the things needed, usually me because I had a car (my sister never obtained a driver's license) was the good one, and the other one was the bad one who never helped. I often wondered why people who were practically strangers to us would start thinking that we had to fulfill all their wishes. Over the years I had found out that there were really no connections between us and that blood is not thicker than water. Our relationship had become or maybe always been superficial, and when I thought of the bad and miserable times and the good times we had, I could only come to the conclusion that there were more bad times than good times. More and more, I thought about leaving it all behind and going back to America to get away from gossip, envy, falsity, and jealousy. The initial reason for moving back to Germany was still a dream awaiting fulfillment.

I still had not found a family, a place where I belonged, people I could trust, and a place I could call home. In the end we had become almost strangers again, knowing now that I could not trust my own family members.

The news over the years always reminded us that the wall still existed, and that people were still being killed trying to overcome it. A big cross on the West part of the wall had all the names written on it of those who had gotten killed in the attempt to escape the communist side. Graffiti all over the ten-foot-high wall showed what people thought about the monster with remarks such as "Honecker [president of the DDR] open the wall!" or "Reunite our brothers and sisters!" The museum at Checkpoint Charlie got bigger and bigger, since the human characteristic of never giving up let people come up with new ideas to find a way to freedom. The longing for freedom became too great for hundreds of people in the beginning of 1989. The news reported from Hungary and Czechoslovakia that people had climbed over the fences of the West German embassies and had requested asylum, filling the yards and the rooms of the embassies. Employees of the embassies pleaded with the people to stop climbing the fences because several children, pushed over the sharp points of the metal spikes, had gotten hurt. Nevertheless, hundreds camped in front of the embassies waiting their turn to get in. The East German police tried to chase them away, arresting some and threatening others with arrests, but were unsuccessful in their attempts to keep them away from the embassies.

I visited my friends again, and we had the same conversations about how nice it would be if I could take Wanda all the way home and have her stay a while. I told her maybe her wish would come true one day soon. They told me that Wanda's niece had escaped through the Hungarian embassy to the West and no one was prepared for it. I had to promise to let them know when I heard from her. Wanda's brother and his wife were devastated and thought they never would see her again. She never had mentioned anything to her family about her plans, having only told them she would go on vacation in Hungary for two weeks. It started happening all over Czechoslovakia and Hungary. More and more people came to the West from these countries other embassies. September came along, and every day we heard the rumors getting louder and louder that the communists were letting people out. Honecker supposedly had agreed to ease the visitation rights between the West and the East and that the border would be opened. No one really believed it since some newspapers reported Honecker saying, "The wall we be there forever." Every day exciting news about another crossing point letting people from the East come into the West put people all over Germany in suspense, and they started to suspect that something big was about to happen. Everyone was wondering; fighting disbelief, hoping, wishing, and waiting for what would come in the days that followed.

THE DAY THE BORDER FELL

The news reported again that another control point had opened, and on November 9, 1989, the unimaginable happened. I looked at the TV in disbelief, it was about 10:30 at night, when a movie camera showed a control point being opened from the East and people over people came storming out of the East. Running, as if they were afraid that they still would be stopped, looking around and back to the control point, and still running. When far enough from the control point, their faces first showed disbelief, but slowly there appeared laughter, tears of happiness, and joy. A reporter interrupted the news saying that Honecker supposedly had decided to open all control points, but it was not confirmed yet. Suddenly everything broke loose. The wall opened everywhere they kept saying. Sonja and I got in the car to get to Friedrich Strasse. We made it to the center of the city, close to the Kurfürsten Damm. Driving became impossible. Everywhere we looked were people and Trabants (the two-cylinder car from the East). It seemed everyone had just one goal—to make it to the Kuh-Damm (the most popular street in West Berlin). Someone said that the police had tried to control all the people by trying to create barriers for the East Germans to be able to get through to the West but were forced very soon to give it up. Every Trabant was greeted with a big "hello" and a friendly knock on its hood. They called it "Trabbi knocking." Suddenly, the huge screen on the Europa Center, usually used for merchandise commercials, showed people getting on top of the wall, started chipping away from it with knifes and sledgehammers and everything they could find. The air was filled with singing, crying, laughter, screaming, and the noise of glasses hitting glasses. Champagne was suddenly available, no one knew where it came from, balloons and confetti were flying through the air, and music appeared out of nowhere. Strangers were hugging each other, laughing, and crying. All over Berlin around the control points, the traffic had come to a standstill, too many people had made traffic impossible. Everywhere you looked you saw happy, crying, unbelieving and astounded faces that still could not get over it that the wall, which had for twenty-eight very long years dominated personal lives, could suddenly become something they could permeate now. After hours and hours of searching and looking for Wanda and Klaus, we went home again around two in the morning. When going to bed, we knew that East Germany and West Germany were slowly melting together again, and we looked forward to a new day and the new beginning.

The "Monster" (the wall) that had hampered the economy and brought death, tears, misery, suspicion, hatred, and discouragement about being unable to change anything was suddenly not important anymore. People still were in total disbelief, afraid that maybe this was only a test and that the wall would be closed again in the coming days. The news reported that Honecker had decided to open the border for better human relations and to better the living conditions of his people. In other words, he admitted that his economy could not support his people anymore, and that after the Hungary and Czechoslovakia incidents, people in East Germany had realized that they had found other ways to escape communism. The urge of the people for freedom could never be suppressed forever, and family ties are stronger than cement. Ingenuity would always come up with new ways to overcome the unthinkable. Berlin, a city of two million, grew over night into a city of almost four million.

United, in the weeks that followed, the East German population stayed visible when they came, with their unmistakable purses and cloth bags to go shopping and their clothing. Plastic bags and pretty wrapped-up goods were unknown to them, as were so many other things. Often I saw them just standing in the stores and just looking (the same as I once did), seeing goods they had only heard of, being astounded at the enormous availability of it all. They were comparing prices and trying to figure out how much their money would buy them. Their currency was at first accepted, but it did not last very long and the West German government made their currency available in a one-to-one exchange. The need to catch up with the times lost became East Germans' first concern. In order to do this, they needed money. That is where the banks stepped in, offering those heretofore unknown credit cards and bank loans. In order to get the economies in the East sector going again, businesses were offered money to open up in the East and stay there for at least a year.

Forty years of communism had resulted in outdated factories, low production, minimal exportation, and almost non-existent upkeep of structural assets. Inside the Dresdner Zwinger (a museum), for example, treasures of the Russian tsar families showed the richness of the empires with jewels, ivory, and gold, but the Dresdner Zwinger itself started to crumble away from pollution and time. All areas where tourists were allowed to go were kept in better condition than the others. It was always shocking to see the poor condition of housing outside tourist areas. One saw butcher shops empty of goods and long lines when news came that a delivery was expected. The grocery stores were close to empty, offering no tropical fruits, coffee, nylons, chocolates, etc. Most of the people from the East, seeing the overwhelming amount of it all in the West, led them to assume that everyone in West was rich. They started to want everything as soon as possible to accommodate their wants and needs. That the people in the West had to work forty years for their standard of living was beyond their comprehension.

With the opening of the border Honecker had put the West German economy in a predicament. Suddenly a feasible way had to be found to bring the East to a high productive level in order to be able to support itself again. That meant investing money for years to build up the economy, create jobs, provide housing, and increase productivity. In order to do so, taxes were raised in the West along with the cost of living, and people needed to be told over and over that it was for a good cause, to bring the two Germanys together again.

It was hard for the individual to see why they had to pay for forty years of mismanagement and misconception by a corrupt government. Everyone in the former East Germany knew that the government officials themselves owned the best properties, had the biggest parties with Western commodities, drove the best Western cars, could travel in any country they liked, and had everything they needed at their disposal. And this was the same government that stopped families from seeing their families in the West. The same government that took away Western merchandise brought to the border for friends and relatives; The same government that denied their people to be informed about what was going on in the rest of the world; The same government that denied their people "luxury" articles such as coffee, nylons, chocolates, magazines, cigarettes, and such simple things as bathroom mats or door handles. Because of the behavior of this government, people in the West had to pay now to correct the mismanagement and corruption.

Another big problem arose with the opening of the border. All the people who had owned houses in the East and had decided to escape, leaving their property, now wanted that property back. Legally, the property belonged to the East German government, and it was rented out to people who had tried their best to keep it up in their spare time, with very hard-to-get materials. They would not know where to go to if they had to move out. Property formerly used for recreation was suddenly bought and restricted for use, lakes were suddenly filled with roaring motor boats, and the serenity of the landscape was ruined by people from the West trying to escape that former island, Berlin. Needless to say, it did not take very long for a sense of rejection to arise on both sides. One side wanted to keep their recreational areas and landscape intact and have everything the West had. They wanted to keep tourism out and for the West to leave their properties alone. The other side was annoyed with having to pay higher taxes, higher cost of living, higher rents, etc., being under the impression they had the right to buy land in the East, enjoy the lakes, and use whatever was worth using. Time went by and the attitude of either side changed, turning the environment almost hostile.

As many times as we had talked about how things would change if the border ever opened, that many times we were wrong about it. Wanda and Klaus were confronted with almost insurmountable problems. Capitalism had caught up with them—they were suddenly put in a position where they had to revise their whole way of living. Never having had to worry under communism about having enough work (the contracts and with it the money was given to them by the government) or getting paid for their work, under capitalism they faced a whole new ball game. Now, they had to find work and bring in money for themselves, and most difficult of all, they had to overhaul the whole business to keep up with Western standards and laws. New machinery, new buildings, new trucks, and more employees were necessary to keep up with the cutthroat competition.

Their work started to play a main role in their lives, making them aware that from now on they had to compete with established companies in the west part of Berlin and West Germany. They had to learn all over again the ways of credit cards, paying on installments, or just not paying at all. Both over fifty, they had to adjust to having to borrow millions, working twelve to sixteen hours a day, hunting for work orders, learn how to advertise their business (which was unnecessary before), competition, and having almost no leisure time. Their son had to go back to the university and change his degree and get a certification to train workers in their company (which he had done before anyway), since the West laws required a different degree to become an instructor. The prospect of inheriting millions in debt after his parents' death placed a dim outlook on his future. To find help with the growing business, he looked unsuccessfully for a loving wife who could help, like his mother, with the administrative part of the business. No, times were not easy ones under capitalism for a lot of people.

Another group of people was dissatisfied: the ones who always had a job under communism, since its biggest claim was that "No one is unemployed under communism." It was common to employ the drinkers, the drug addicts, and those who did not like to work. Often when we went shopping in the East, before the border came down, we had to wait in the stores to be served. Sales personnel stood talking and laughing together and ignored the customers, knowing they would not be fired for their behavior. Now the same people could not find any jobs and had to go on welfare. The unemployment compensation drove up the unemployment rate, and also drained the West government's money supply. Overall, the situation in the West was not very comforting. The realization that sacrifices had to be made day after day to get the economy in the East going again, in order to be self-supporting one day, started a wave of discontentment. Youth groups from the East, such as the Skinheads, used this discontentment as an excuse to riot and indulge in disorderly conduct, blaming the government for unemployment, dictatorship, and limiting their freedom of expression. Berlin's Kuhdamm, which had been an exclusive street for tourism, exclusive restaurants, and shops, soon became the main street for hooligans and rebel marches. The hooligans and rebels settled down in condemned buildings in Kreuzberg, where the working class lived, claiming that housing was available so why not use it. Windows were shot with black sheets or cardboard, graffiti written all over the buildings, condemning the West government for not given people work and housing. A whole street block was turned into their domain, with police cars standing by day and night.

Apartments, which had before the fall of the border, rented for 700 Deutsche Marks, rented suddenly for 1,200 Deutsche Marks, forcing many people to look for more affordable housing.

The rising cost of living, the nonexistent ties with the family, and a big event for Sonja played a big role in my decision to leave Berlin and move back to America. For Sonja the move came earlier than expected by anyone.

A WEDDING

When Sonja was ten, she went with both of her cousins to a summer camp in Trier. There she got to know a German boy and his sister. They played together, and when the camp was over, the German boy kept in contact with her. Her German was not very good then, but that was exactly what was so fascinating for Ray. He came to visit often and seemed mesmerized by everything American: food, toys, language, and especially Sonja. He thought it was beautiful, funny, and interesting when she tried to speak German to him. Soon she was introduced to his family and went several times to spend a night with his sister, Tara. She liked it even though the boy's mother was in the middle of an ugly divorce, living off the government and going out often leaving the children by themselves (which I didn't find out much later).

Years went by with the friendship being nonexistent and then flaring up again. Sonja was sixteen when Ray started to show up again and wanted to start dating her. I put a stop to it, allowing only movie visits, dinner invitations at my house, or visiting his family. Sonja started to like Ray more and more and was really hurt when he started dating another American girl who could not speak German very well. That did not seem to work out, and soon he was back trying to convince Sonja that he loved her and he wanted to marry her. Since everyone knew that his only goal consisted of getting to America, her friends and I rejected that idea emphatically, but we were unsuccessful in our pleading with her not to marry him.

I had to realize that I could not do anything to prevent that marriage and came to the decision to make it a very nice memory for her. Knowing his fondness for America, I rented a white Cadillac and an American facility and arranged for American food mixed with German food for the festivities. His mother helped with the financial part of it, a beautiful wedding dress was bought, and on October 19, 1990, she said yes in front of a preacher in a German church. I wanted to give her the wedding I had never had, something to remember for years to come. Tears fell aplenty. The only one from my family attending was my aunt, since it was no-talking time again with the rest of them. Wanda and Klaus were not invited because Ray did not like them at all and did not want them there. Klaus had the audacity to tell Ray right to his face that he was unrealistic, without having a job or any work experience moving to a strange country. He had asked Ray how he wanted support his new wife in America and also mentioned that America didn't have the German welfare system, which could be easily abused. Ray just brushed it off and told him he did not know what he was talking about. After that conversation he never wanted to go back with us to see Klaus and Wanda. Ray also did not want to keep his family name, Herrmann, since we told him about the nutty PeeWee Hermann, and took on Sonja's family name. Since Sonja was an American citizen, the paperwork to go to America did not take long, and a couple of months later, I had to take her to the airport to say goodbye for an undetermined time. I could not believe it; everything went too fast. I lost my daughter for the third time, only this time I knew that her future looked very unsure and maybe unsafe. I was alone again, and the letters from Sonja convinced me that I needed to hurry to get everything organized to leave Germany also. I started selling everything again, got my passport renewed, arranged for a flight to Texas where Sonja and Ray lived now and another August came along to bring a big event into my life.

The whole family suddenly acted as if they were going to miss me very much, saying I should not make the big move: I was too old, all my family was in Germany, and I was going to regret it. I knew better, the only person I hated leaving was Wanda. We promised to stay in contact and vowed that she surely would come and visit one day ("When I get my bachelor's degree," she said). A tearful goodbye from my sister at the airport, and off I went, back to America. I suddenly could not wait anymore to get back again to the place where I had felt at home for the first time in my life: Texas, the place I had stayed the longest ever, the place where I had had the best times in my life (St. Edward's), and the place where I could achieve something for myself. The climate and the people were a lot friendlier, the pace was slower, and housing was affordable. I remembered a medium-size city, traffic being friendly, people leaving their doors open when leaving to go shopping, and being able to buy a nice three-bedroom home for about $35,000. That was at the end of the seventies or early eighties.

mewhere else someone
n worse than me. That
ed into death, that bad
m had turned into fatal
to renew my strengths
me worse off than me
the root always a turn to
g hope to begin again
the teacher of life is
f the people untold

HOME AGAIN

It was 1992. I had heard from Sonja that she had left Ray and had moved in with her new boyfriend. She got to know him when she worked at the post office. She was in love again, and I was pleased by what she had written about him. He seemed to be a lot more mature than Ray, and he was taking good care of her.

I had flown from Berlin to Chicago and then to Austin. I could not believe my eyes when coming in for a landing. The skyline of Austin looked almost as though I were flying into Berlin. It was astounding and beautiful. Tired from the flight, I was wide awake when landing in Austin and had a beautiful feeling of finally being home again. I had to hold back not to bend down and kiss the ground when coming out of the plane. It was an overwhelming feeling. When I saw my daughter again after two years, the tears just came. No one could have been happier than I was at that moment. When we finally let go of each other, she introduced me to her boyfriend, and I was pleased with what I saw. A forty-five-minute trip out to Spicewood gave me the chance to talk a little to both of them, realizing my English had really gotten bad in the twelve years of not speaking much.

The next morning, struggling with jet lag, we had

a chance to catch up with what had happened in our lives. My daughter had gotten an apartment for me in Austin and had furnished it with rented furniture, so we were not in a hurry to get there. We talked for hours—her boyfriend was at work—when I realized we were in the country, with nothing around but fields, hills, and a dog and a cat. His parents, who lived in a trailer on the other end of the property, owned the property. Kenny, my daughter's boyfriend, lived with her in the house his grandparents had lived in. He was divorced and had one son. He wanted to get a trailer also but needed a septic tank installed first. It was very quiet and peaceful, and we enjoyed the day together.

Later that day I wanted two things only, to see Austin and St. Edward's again and to find out how it all had changed. Sonja drove me around. We stopped at St. Edward's, and the same feeling I had at the airport overwhelmed me when I stood in front of the main building overlooking the skyline of Austin. I was home. A sense of satisfaction and relief, as after a long wandering and searching, settled over me. After that, Sonja took me to my new apartment, and I was very pleased and thankful for the way she had arranged everything for my arrival. She had to go back to work the next day, and I wanted to get a newspaper for my job search, open a bank account, and buy a car. The thickness and size of the Sunday paper quickly made me aware that Austin was not a medium-size city anymore.

When I had left Germany, I had set myself three goals: to buy a little house again (it was impossible in Germany to buy a house for less than 500,000 Deutsche Marks), finish my degree from St. Edward's University, and maybe find a partner for the rest of my life. Since I had had to work all my life, after one month went by, I got nervous because I had not found a job yet. All my experience I had was in Germany, my English was not very good anymore, and being fifty did not help either. Instead of being patient and searching longer, I took a job at the Austin airport as a security officer for Southwest Airlines for $4.25 an hour, working from 4:20 a.m. till 2:30 p.m. I started looking for a little house, and in December, 1993, I moved into a little two-bedroom, 1 bath in a nice neighborhood in South Austin. My first goal was achieved.

Now I had to start working on my second goal: to finish my halted education in 1980. I met with people at the new college program (a program for adult students at St. Edward's) and returned in 1994, taking six hours and working full time. In order to reduce the cost of a St. Edward's education, I managed to take some classes at Austin Community College. My enthusiasm about finishing my degree started to inspire my daughter also. I started asking around whether she could use the GI Bill from her father, since she was the daughter of a veteran killed in active duty. We were told yes, but only until she turned twenty-six. That left her two years to get an associate's degree. Her boyfriend was very supportive and encouraged her, telling her she did not have to work, just to go to school. Both of us worked on our degrees and always said that it would be nice to finish at the same time. This became reality when on May 9, 1997, she received her Associate Degree in Biology, and on May 10, 1997, I received my bachelor of liberal studies. On May 2, we had picked up Klaus and Wanda from the

Dallas airport who were the only German friends celebrating with us.

In the three years since I had started back at St. Edward's, I had changed jobs in order to better my income and was then working for $9 per hour at a part-time job at Austin Community College. I took my first two-week vacation for Klaus and Wanda's visit, and after the commencement celebrations, we went traveling to South Padre Island, to NASA in Houston, to San Antonio and the Alamo and the river walk, Buchanan Dam, and to Sea World. Even though it was just May and to me not very hot, both suffered from the heat. Passing the biggest ranch in Texas on Highway 71, my German friends couldn't believe that long, long stretch of highway. The width and the overall size of Texas amazed them again and again. When driving on Highway 71 through Kingsville, both could not believe that for hours and hours there was nothing but a straight road, no houses, nothing. The emptiness of the landscape convinced them fast that carrying a cellular phone was a necessity and not a luxury. Klaus, being an engineer, was again and again astonished about the grandeur of the intertwining highway bridges, the (in Germany unthinkable) wood construction of homes, and the abundance of churches. They also were amazed on how seemingly unorganized the location of businesses or homes appeared, about the thousands of signs and billboards on the sides of the road, and the way the Americans ate. I showed them my Texas, the way we live and celebrate, and the friendly Texan way of life. They stocked up on jeans, cowboy hats, clothes, and souvenirs, and on the nineteenth of May, we had to take them, heavy hearted, back to Dallas.

Our lives went back to the daily routine, and I was determined to find a job at St. Edward's. I wanted to give back to the university I loved and work there as long as they let me. I had to learn again not to put my expectations too high. I thought that now that I had my degree it would be easier to find something that paid a lot better. When a job was offered I applied, but over and over again I received letters saying that the position had been filled. I was about to give up, when finally I was called in for an interview for a position I had applied for. After a year of applying over and over for different jobs within the university, I realized that a degree does not necessarily open doors more easily. Two facts seemed to count against me: no relevant job experience in America and my age. My German background, being unfamiliar with making a lot of contacts and networking, also hampered my efforts.

Sonja, on the other hand, found what she already liked to do in high school, a job in an accounting department in a big hotel. She enjoyed her colleagues, her environment, and being close to her home.

The only thing wrong was that both of us seemed to be without luck when it came to men. Sonja had broken off with Kenny, realizing that a fifteen-year age difference was too much, and had started seeing a younger, Hispanic man. I had broken off, after two years with an older gentleman I was seeing, whom I had let move in with me. Neither of us was very lucky with partners, seeming to get to know only the ones who were wrong for us.

I heard from Germany every now and then. The ties are gotten loose, and the times in-between phone calls and letters gotten longer. My older daughter started to get in contact with my real mother, and started visiting her. I found out from her that she married a physicist in May 1997 and separated three months later from him. She had to wait one year under German law before starting divorce proceedings and had started them now. I do not know details, since our interaction evolved into a friend-to-friend relationship, not into a mother-and-daughter one.

It was around Thanksgiving when I suddenly got a card from my sister who was in Ft. Mayers in Florida. She had gotten an invitation from her "best friend" to stay with her for a while, but when she got there, she couldn't stay there and was forced to stay in a hotel for two weeks. She wanted me to come and stay with her a couple of days. I had started the a new job at St. Edward's, so taking vacation already was impossible, and getting airline tickets around Thanksgiving was another problem. We could only talk on the phone now and then. She was here with her favored daughter Katja. Her other daughter had moved out into an apartment in Berlin and was not married. She did her apprenticeship as a saleslady, and her favored daughter studied to become a registered pediatric nurse, and was still living with her.

My real mother will turn eighty the next year, and she would be happy if we came to see her in Switzerland for that occasion I was told. My stepfather just spent three weeks in his home country, Italy, with his family. When he got back, my mother and he decided to leave for another two weeks to Germany to see Wanda and Klaus.

Time has lapsed, my graduate studies will come to an end in May 2002, my parents are in France right now for three weeks with my stepfather's sister, and my daughter got married again and has a fifteen-month-old boy she had always wanted. She finally found her "good husband and father," and I gave up on ever achieving my third goal.

WHAT'S NEXT?

Was this my life? I often wondered. Forced to overcome and searching for something that was in me all the time. Life had turned me into a fugitive, a wanderer, a mother, an artist, a writer, and a survivor. Stronger than ever before, I look at my daughters and hoped that they will never have to go through similar experiences. Times are different, circumstances are different, but one thing never changes: unless everyone finds inner strength, inner home, and inner self-love, they will never find fulfillment. All the searching for love, all the longing for belonging, all the wanting for a home, it always was right here, in me. Every human being that has touched my life, influenced it, shared it with me for a while, tried to form it and tried to dominate it brought me a step closer to myself. To a person that had seen misery, death, unfairness, sickness, unlawfulness, love, kindness, and met other survivors. It just took a very rocky road, and a very long time to come to the conclusion that I could find anything I was looking for within myself. That the strength to overcome, to survive, to forgive, and to love again was inside of me the whole time. I thank all the persons who touched my life in one time or another, bringing me one step closer on the way to finding another piece of the puzzle called life. Peaceful with my surrounding and me, life has become what I always wanted it to be. Loving the every-day challenges of a demanding job, and coming home to a loving surrounding, I often ask myself, *What else is necessary?* I even overcame the stigma of being a single woman, the societies pondering about not being normal when choosing to live my life alone, since I know that there is absolutely nothing wrong with me psychologically or physically. I was allowed to do what I loved best, learning. Thankful every day for being alive, I keep telling myself that destiny had written all the lines for me and brought me to this place, so I will patiently wait for the next chapter to be written …

EPILOGUE

Throughout these essays, I have tried to describe events in my life and to reflect on their significance. This has been no small task because as I kept sorting through my experiences I was also searching to find points of misunderstandings or tension within myself that I might resolve on the page. I was, in truth, a woman who searched for a meaningful life. But events in my life were hardly ever calm; therefore, they have not been easy to recall and assess.

I often feel compelled, when looking back, to celebrate having conquered walls of torture, brainwashing, death, fear, and suspicion to celebrate the escape from my detrimental surroundings, confronting new ideals, political systems, and cultures.

As these memoirs have served the purpose of finding insights and closure for my own good, I hope that the readers can identify with some of the events, and that these can help them also to unravel hard times in their own lives, perhaps bringing closure and a measure of contentment.

Often in my life, I was asked where I had gotten the strengths to carry on and not give up. I thought about it and it occurred to me that every time something bad, dangerous, sad, or painful had happened in my life the thoughts occurred to me that somewhere else someone else is experiencing something even worse than me. That danger for someone else had turned into death, that bad had turned into worse and that pain had turned into fatal illness and so on. It helped me a lot to renew my strengths and faith telling myself that others are worse of than me and I should be thankful that my life took always a turn to the next chapter, which would bring hope to begin again.

I once read somewhere that the teacher of life is pain—under his breath, the souls of the people unfold.

WORKS CONSULTED

Barrington, Judith. *Writing the Memoir.* 2nd ed. Portland, OR: The Eighth Mountain Press, 2002.

Bernays, Anne, and Pamela Painter. *What If?* New York, NY: Addison-Wesley Longman Publishers, 1995.

Bunnin, Brad & Peter Beren. *The Writer's Legal Companion.* 3rd ed. Reading, MA: Perseus Books, 1998.

Clark, Thomas. *Queries & Submissions.* Cincinnati, OH: Writer's Digest Books, 1995.

Dillard, Annie. *The Writing Life.* New York, NY: HarperCollins Publishers, Inc., 1989.

Dillard, Annie, and Cort Conley, eds. *Modern American Memoirs.* New York, NY: HarperCollins Publishers, Inc., 1995.

Fry, Patricia L. *The Nonfiction Book Proposal: Put Your Best Foot Forward.* Google, Austin, 20 Jan. 2006. http://www.writing-world.com/publish/proposal.shtml

Funder, Anna. *Stasiland: True stories from Behind the Berlin Wall.* Google, Austin, 2 Feb. 2006. http://www.popmatters.com/books/reviews/s/stasiland.shtml

Hacker, Diana. *A Writer's Reference.* 5th ed. Bedford St. Martin's, 2003.

Hensel, Jana. *After the Wall: Confessions from an East German Childhood and the Life that Came Next.* Trans. Jefferson Chase. Google, Austin, 10 Jan. 2006. http://www.publicaffairsbooks.com/publicaffairsbooks-cgi-in/display?book=1586482661

Holm, Kirsten C., et al., eds. *Writer's Market.* Cincinnati, OH: Writer's Digest Books, 1998.

Roorbach, Bill. *Writing Life Stories.* Cincinnati, OH: Story Press, 1998.

Sample Book Proposals. Google, Austin, 23 Feb. 2006. http://www.writing-world.com/publish/samples.shtml

Shimberg, Elaine F. *Write Where You Live: Successful Freelancing at Home.* Cincinnati, OH: Writer's Digest Books, 1999.

Sprenger, Heinrich, and Irene Charlotte Streul. *VON DER SPALTUNG ZUR EINHEIT:* 1945–1990 Eine Deutsche Chronik in Texten und Bildern. Korb, Germany: Press and Information Office of the Federal Government, 1992.

WORKS CITED

Luuk, Ernst. *East Berlin.* 1st ed. Informationszentrum Berlin: FAB-Verlag, Berlin, Germany, 1988.

Ramm, Frederik. A sign on a door in the Wall saying "this door is defective, please use next." Google, Austin, 1 March, 2006.http://www.remote.org/frederik/culture/berlin/imglist.html

License

All photos on these pages are my intellectual property. Their re-use is allowed under the following terms:

if you earn money with my photos, e.g. by including them on a CD-ROM you sell, then you must include this URL as a source link in the collection or the accompanying material: **http://www.remote.org/frederik/culture/berlin/** everybody else may do as he or she likes, but of course I'm happy if you refer to the above URL as a source.

Ullrich,Klaus., et al., *DDR.* 3rd ed. Leipzig, DDR: Druckerei Fortschritt Erfurt, 1997.

Ziethen, Horst. *Die neue und historische Hauptstadt Berlin und Potsdam im Farbbild.* Ziethen-Panorama Verlag, Berlin, 1999.

OME AGAIN 211
AT'S NEXT? 219
EPILOGUE 221
ONSULTED 223
RKS CITED 225